The creative professional

The creative professional:
Learning to teach 14–19-year-olds

Edited by Kate Ashcroft and David James

FALMER PRESS
Taylor & Francis Group

First published 1999 by Falmer Press
11 New Fetter Lane, London EC4P 4EE

Simultaneously published in the USA and Canada
by Garland Inc., 19 Union Square West, New York, NY 10003

Falmer Press is an imprint of the Taylor & Francis Group

Typeset in Melior by Graphicraft Limited, Hong Kong
Printed and bound in Great Britain by TJ International Ltd, Padstow,
Cornwall

British Library Cataloguing in Publication Data
A catalogue record for this book is available from the British Library

Library of Congress Cataloging in Publication Data
The creative professional : learning to teach 14–19-year-olds / edited
  by Kate Ashcroft and David James.
      p.   cm.
    Includes bibliographical references and index.
    1. High school teachers—Great Britain.   2. High school teachers—
Training of—Great Britain.   3. High school teaching—Great
Britain.   4. Creative thinking—Study and teaching (Secondary)—
Great Britain.   I. Ashcroft, Kate.   II. James, David, 1956–   .
    LB1777.4.G72C74   1999
    371.1′00941—dc21   99–28168
                                                                          CIP

ISBN 0-7507-0740-2

Contents

List of figures

Chapter 1

Introduction

David James and *Kate Ashcroft*

Why should teachers be interested in *creativity* in relation to their work? One answer comes from the government's Green Paper (*The Learning Age – A Renaissance for a New Britain*) which appeared in February 1998:

> ❝ *The Industrial Revolution was built on capital investment in plant and machinery, skills and hard physical labour . . . The information and knowledge-based revolution of the twenty-first century will be built on a very different foundation – investment in the intellect and creativity of people.* (DfEE, 1998a, p. 9)

This and a host of similar statements leave little doubt that teachers are now central to the well-being of the society and the economy. Yet at the same time, the 1990s have not been a particularly happy or rewarding period for teachers as a professional group. In schools they have had to contend with almost continual reform of the curriculum and assessment; in further education they have faced fundamental changes in the nature of their work, in funding regimes and in contracts of employment. In the preparation of teachers, regulations have shifted the balance away from 'theory' and towards 'practice' (Hoyle and John, 1995) and there have been wholesale changes in the specification of the curriculum and in the measurement of competence and standards. The most common justification for such educational reforms is the raising of standards (though in practice this can mean many things and begs many further questions). Importantly, many reforms have occurred in a climate of consumerism, marketisation and increased accountability and have either reduced professional autonomy or *appeared* to do so. Many teachers have been left feeling that the rewards and recognition they receive are not commensurate with the value of their work to society. A second answer to the question about interest in creativity is that many teachers are interested in rebuilding their confidence, in rediscovering their autonomy to make decisions and in exploring the alternatives open to them in their teaching.

This is a book *for* teachers. This seems an obvious point to make until one looks at many of the books available under the general umbrella of education: these often turn out to be *about* teachers, teaching, teacher education, learning, thinking, the curriculum, schools, colleges and educational policy, amongst other things. The vast majority of this work and the research underpinning it is sound and of intrinsic interest, with considerable importance for teachers. Yet many teachers find it difficult to 'translate' the insights in terms of their own practice. This difficulty is usually portrayed as a problem of communication or dissemination, or as a rift between theory and practice, or taken to be evidence of inappropriate research agendas or even poor quality research. Yet it is not necessarily any of these things. Much more likely is that the difficulty arises from the nature of professional knowledge itself, where the type of knowledge generated by well-planned research studies will often – by definition – appear as far removed from the context the individual teacher knows well, or it will seem remote from many of the day-to-day dilemmas and decisions that are of real concern to the teacher in a school or college. This book takes most of its examples from the United Kingdom (UK). Nevertheless, we have tried to single out issues that will have relevance to teachers and student teachers in a variety of contexts and countries.

One tried-and-tested solution to the problem is to encourage teachers themselves to be researchers. Indeed, this book may be thought of as arising from a modern interpretation of the *teacher as researcher* tradition. It is a collection of chapters covering different aspects of the work of the teacher in a school or college. They are united by an invitation to consider the meaning of creativity in some of the major tasks of teaching, to look at the nature of teaching as professional work, and to encourage the carrying out of useful enquiry in and around professional practices, assumptions and contexts. Whilst it is aimed primarily at beginning teachers, the book will also be of interest to professional tutors and mentors involved in a range of teacher education programmes including (in the UK) secondary BA/BSc/BEd and PGCE, and Cert Ed (FE)/PGCE in post-compulsory education. It will also be of interest to those who are still at an early stage in their teaching career. It is an attempt to provide ideas, inspiration, suggestions about processes and other kinds of support for teachers to help them to tackle some of the many challenges that they face. It is not an attempt to be comprehensive, and there are many parts of the role that are not singled out for attention.

In many places the book makes reference to relevant published research or other source material. However, it is primarily driven by the distillation of experiences. Some of these are the experiences of the authors themselves, but the authors also drew on the experiences of hundreds of teachers with whom they have worked, especially through various parts of the *Modular Programme for Continuing Professional Development* in the Faculty of Education at the University of the West of England, Bristol. The teachers studying towards various awards on this programme work in a wide range of educational settings, many of them with young people in the 14–19 age-range. Several modules in the programme are structured so as to promote systematic reflection and opportunities to plan change for the teacher, often with outcomes of a highly practical nature. As an example, a module that was first offered in 1991 entitled *Creative Teaching and Learning Strategies* sets out to provide the conditions for some quite rapid professional development via a three-stage process. The module was spread across a series of evening group meetings and included plenty of opportunity for discussion in a supportive atmosphere. Firstly, participants would try to locate their own, habitual assumptions about learning and teaching in a process akin to drawing a conceptual map, sometimes making use of a *personal constructs* activity and through the use of a range of well-known writings on learning, teaching and related concepts. Secondly, they would attempt to identify a number of gaps between their current practices and what they could argue were more desirable practices. These gaps could be characterised as strengths and weaknesses in relation to some of the more established ideas about better or worse teaching; or they could be sorted or ranked in terms of the opportunities they appeared to offer. For example, some would allow scope for the teacher to effect change (either individually or in conjunction with colleagues), whilst others would seem beyond the teacher's control and related to structural, cultural or resource issues where the teacher's influence was minimal. The third stage required participants to produce a design for innovation in an area of their teaching or related work. In some cases they were able to 'go live' with this in the workplace, incorporating a review of their experimentation with some sort of measurement of the degree of success they had; in other cases, timing did not allow for this level of evaluation and participants simply presented their designs as action plans. The three-stages were close to many characterisations of learning as a cyclical process, an idea that is taken up later in this book.

Running this module and our work as teachers and with teachers have left a number of impressions, including:

1   that on the whole, teachers prefer a short and eclectic consideration of learning theories and contexts rather than being given a rounded introduction to the current state of disciplines such as the psychology of learning or the sociology of education, provided they could follow up particular lines of interest;

2   that even the most well-read and experienced teachers do not want to be left entirely to their own devices to relate concepts to their own work-place, or in locating, or mapping, their own assumptions and practices;

3   that even experienced teachers can, like their novice counterparts, become hampered by thinking that they have got to be original and imaginative in every lesson they teach, but can also fall into a trap of under-estimating their creative potential (see Halliwell, 1993, p. 68);

4   that contrary to the findings of a number of different pieces of research (Desforges, 1995), in the right circumstances busy professionals are keen to learn from experience and put a great deal of effort into engaging with activities clearly designed to make them *less* rather than more comfortable in the short-term, provided they believe that they might 'know themselves better' at the end of the process. To a considerable degree, impressions like these have influenced the shape and content of this book.

In modern societies, virtually everyone has been to school and been taught by more than one teacher. It is sometimes said that this is why everyone considers themselves an expert on educational matters. Expert or not, views on the quality of teachers and teaching can be heard all the time, from parents, politicians, pupils and students, the media and teachers themselves, to say nothing of the agencies which governments and others set up for the express purpose of measuring the quality of teaching. Although the idea that teachers are 'born and not made' is still popular, the way in which teachers have been trained or educated is widely thought to be the most crucial variable in how good they are at their job (see for example Millett, 1997). In recent years in the UK, a great deal of money has been spent on devising and policing standards for initial teacher education courses for school teachers, and similar moves are afoot in relation to Further Education (FE) teachers. Current UK government initiatives seek to resolve a recruitment crisis and acknowledge the need to attract and then retain more of the young people who appear at present to be choosing other professions over teaching (see, for instance, DfEE, 1998b).

Most teachers of the 14–19 age-range will have undergone a specialist preparation of some sort at some stage. At the end of this period they will have been certified as having reached an acceptable standard to practise on their own. Yet for all its simple appeal, this idea (of being trained once-and-for-all) is fundamentally flawed in the case of a job as complex and change-ridden as teaching. It makes far more sense to see the knowledge involved in teaching as a process which, though it will hopefully grow rapidly to reach an agreed standard in a period of initial teacher education, should never be considered as 'finished' – at least not until a teacher retires! This 'process' view of knowledge connects directly with another idea – that of *reflective pedagogy* – which permeates the *Continuing Professional Development Programme* mentioned above and which also permeates this book. In using this term, we move beyond the rather impoverished definition of reflective practice promoted by the Teacher Training Agency (TTA) as evidence-based practice focused on outcomes (Cordingley, 1998). Ours is a much more complex and sophisticated model that incorporates enquiry as one of its processes, but also ethical and values dimensions; long- as well as short-term considerations; a recognition of the dilemmas inherent in complex human interactions; and a focus on empowerment of students and teachers (see for instance, Ashcroft and Foreman-Peck, 1994).

The rest of the book is divided into nine chapters. Chapter 2 presents an exploration of some major notions of creativity in relation to teaching, linking together a number of different interpretations and making a connection with the idea of critical thinking. The chapter ends with a sketch of a notion of *professional creativity*. Chapter 3 discusses the idea of being a creative teacher through the conscious adoption of a model of reflective practice. It provides a set of tools for analysing your implicit theories of teaching and other influences on your actions, so that you can conceptualise them in new ways to create transformational solutions to problems. Chapter 4 focuses on teaching methods and the ways in which choices of method may be made using different criteria. In relation to different concepts of learning, it argues for a creative use of learning theories in preference to adherence to one or another of them. In Chapter 5 the teacher's use of groups is considered and guidance is offered on the tasks necessary to make groups function well. It also considers issues as practical as room layout before providing three case studies to illustrate the imaginative use of groups for different purposes. This is followed by Chapter 6 that looks at assessment. The main qualifications for 14–19-year-olds are given brief attention before turning to an important distinction between methods and purposes of assessment and other fundamental concepts. The chapter moves on to examine some deeper understandings of assessment for the insights they might offer the teacher who wishes to be more creative. It is suggested that most of the opportunities to be creative lie in the management of relationships between teachers, learners and the curriculum. Chapter 7 gives an account of relevant meanings of the term 'professional'. It also considers the role and nature of professional knowledge before moving on to look at how these link to values and the collegiate task of being a teacher and a life-long learner who may experience a variety of career trajectories. Chapter 8 presents an introduction to a series of management concepts and issues that can give the relative newcomer to an educational institution several useful 'ideas' for understanding their surroundings and finding ways to act creatively within them. Chapter 9 offers insights into the actions that the creative professional may take to promote social justice and educational opportunity. It explores issues such as the hidden curriculum, empowerment and quality. Finally, Chapter 10 looks at the role of enquiry in the development of the creative professional as a reflective practitioner. It provides a basic introduction to some methods of enquiry, their strengths and weaknesses and ways of assessing research, including ethical issues.

In keeping with an overall aim to 'open up' thinking, considerable care has been taken to write in an accessible style. Where appropriate, chapters present the reader with Enquiry tasks, illustrative examples in the form of Case studies, and sections entitled Reflection where it seems particularly helpful to draw out an experience or a reaction to a particular point. Each chapter also carries brief suggestions for Further reading.

References

ASHCROFT, K. and FOREMAN-PECK, L. (1994) *Managing Teaching and Learning in Further and Higher Education*, London: Falmer Press.

CORDINGLEY, P. (1998) 'Constructing and critiquing reflective practice', *Occasional Paper for TTA Publications Unit*, London: Teacher Training Agency.

DESFORGES, C. (1995) 'How does experience affect theoretical knowledge for teaching?' *Learning and Instruction*, **5**, pp. 385–400.

DfEE (1998a) *The Learning Age – A Renaissance for a New Britain*, London: The Stationery Office, Cm 3790.

DfEE (1998b) *Teachers: Meeting the Challenge*, Sudbury: DfEE Publications.

HALLIWELL, S. (1993) 'Teacher creativity and teacher education' in BRIDGES, D. and KERRY, T. (eds) *Developing Teachers Professionally*, London: Routledge.

HOYLE, E. and JOHN, P.D. (1995) *Professional Knowledge and Professional Practice*, London: Cassell.

MILLETT, A. (1997) 'We cannot settle for second class', *The Times*, 27 June.

Chapter 2

What does it mean to be creative?

David James

Introduction

What is creativity, and what does it have to do with the work of the teacher? It may be helpful to begin by drawing a basic distinction. There seem to be two common interpretations of creativity when looking at teaching and learning. The first, *experiential creativity*, refers to the nurturing of creativity in learners. In some schools and colleges this is seen as a goal for all learners in all curriculum areas, whilst in others it is seen as the business of subjects such as art, drama and English and perhaps design and technology. The second, *professional creativity*, refers to the idea that *being creative as a teacher* is a professional concern or responsibility. Recent research into teachers' views of creativity suggests that both individuals and whole schools can vary a great deal on these and other dimensions in terms of the notions of creativity they hold (Ashworth, 1998).

For present purposes, the focus is on the second interpretation, on *professional creativity*. This is taken to include a desire to develop the creativity of learners. Getting our learners to be creative is sometimes cited as a goal in books about teaching, though the focus is most often on primary education. Marilyn Fryer's book *Creative Teaching and Learning* (Fryer, 1996) is a good example of this. She used a large survey, involving interviews with teachers and theoretical material on creativity, to ascertain ways in which learners' creativity may be nurtured and to explore the reasons for a seeming lack of creativity in education. The issue of teachers themselves developing their own creativity is mentioned but not addressed in Fryer's book. Indeed, the final chapter begins by lamenting the fact that many teachers and lecturers do not see themselves as creative people. In another work which draws to some extent on Fryer's book, Beetlestone reiterates the point that 'Since the inception of a legislated curriculum in this country, creativity has not received the focus it deserves. The time is now ripe for a return to recognizing the central importance of creativity to learning' (Beetlestone, 1998, p. 8). She goes on to provide a comprehensive treatment of various dimensions of creativity in the primary setting. Although the main focus is with the creativity of learners, Beetlestone often argues that teachers also stand to gain a great deal from placing more emphasis on creativity.

One of the main purposes of this book is to suggest how you can be creative yourself in your practice as a teacher. It is about the ways in which creativity has something to say about pedagogy, about the preparations and practices associated with effective work in the classroom. In this chapter I introduce a range of possible definitions of the term 'creativity' and try to suggest their potential relevance for the teacher or lecturer working with young people. The chapter begins with a brief look at two traditional approaches in which creativity is associated with rare talent and divergent thinking, respectively. I then look at a general approach to creativity which attempts to encompass common features as well as educational implications, before turning to a model of the creative process, derived from the writing of Arthur Koestler, which identifies principles that apply to fields as diverse as art, science and humour. Finally, I look at the related concept of critical thinking. The chapter ends with a discussion of the nature of a professional notion of creativity.

Creativity, genius and divergent thinking

Many books have been written about creativity, and there seems to be a particular concentration of them in the late 1950s and early 1960s. However, most seem to have been written by and for psychologists whose interests fall into the general areas of personality, individual differences and cognition. There is a tendency to focus on the 'greatest minds' and on 'gifted' children, and together these features mean that the books are not necessarily of immediate use to teachers and others who might want to use the concepts for examining everyday practices – their own or other peoples.'

In the introduction to a well-used edited collection of articles on creativity, Vernon states:

> *The major, though by no means sole, emphasis [of this book] is on differences between individuals in the abilities and personality characteristics that underlie the production of artistic or scientific work which is generally recognized as creative and original. What various kinds of talents can be distinguished, and, perhaps, measured? What are their origins? What promotes and what hinders their development?*
>
> (Vernon, 1970, pp. 9–10)

The first part of Vernon's collection is entitled 'Pioneer Empirical Studies' and it contains a summary of Sir Francis Galton's *Hereditary Genius* of 1869 along with two other seminal accounts of the possible factors that distinguish eminent people (usually men) from the rest of the people. Galton was Charles Darwin's famous cousin and is an important figure in the history of the development of statistical techniques. Quantification and individual differences were two of his main fascinations, but it is for his invention of *Eugenics* that he is most often remembered by non-specialists. Galton coined this term in 1883 and it referred to his campaign to place restrictions on who should marry whom and on how many children they should be allowed to have, on the grounds of retaining or improving the quality of particular 'races'. The later use of these ideas in fascist regimes and elsewhere is now legendary (see for example Gould, 1981, for a fascinating – though disturbing – account of the history of intelligence testing and its linkage to personal and political interests and motives).

Apart from its historical curiosity value, it is just possible that some teachers would find material like Galton's *Hereditary Genius* helpful in working out how they might best help the brightest of their students, or deal with some of the needs of a specialist class of gifted individuals. Yet, as is clear from all this, the major interests and concerns of such psychologists differ from those of most teachers, whose bread-and-butter work includes dealing with a whole range of capabilities, motivations, interests and backgrounds. Discussions of the characteristics of the most 'celebrated minds' is likely to have a rather limited utility.

The teacher interested in finding creative solutions to some of the everyday problems and challenges of their work may not in any case have the time or the inclination to dig for the sort of insights promised by this type of psychological literature. Furthermore, the apparent preoccupation with underlying (or possible) causes of creativity seems to relegate activity (like making choices, decisions, planning, producing good resources, working well with colleagues) to second place, as surface phenomena. To propose a deep-seated psychological characteristic as causal is to propose some sort of independent variable, genetic or otherwise, which might govern the capacity to teach more or less effectively. The quality and effectiveness of the teaching itself becomes a 'dependent variable', that is to say an effect of something else assumed to be deeper and much more mysterious. It is locked away, and only specialists have some of the keys that might one day unlock it for us. All this has the effect of disempowering teachers, whilst seeming to indicate scientific answers to their questions. In contrast, I would suggest that it is precisely the area of their own choices, decisions and actions that is likely to be of most interest and relevance to teachers.

Related psychological work which is likely to be of more use is the development of tests of thinking skills that go beyond the traditional, convergent tests such as those used in most items within standardised tests of the so-called Intelligence Quotient (which anticipate one correct answer to each problem in a series). Vernon notes that Guilford's work (for example Guilford, 1957) inspired a new direction in this field in the form of attempts to devise tests of divergent thinking: the ability to devise new and original solutions to a problem. Ideas such as these may well be helpful to the teacher who is examining their own practice.

Enquiry task: Thinking divergently

Firstly, list as many uses as you can in one minute for the following items: (a) a paperclip; (b) a brick; (c) a glass of water. Ask someone else to do the same, and compare your lists. Compare the *number* of suggestions, how they *differ*, and also how *unusual* they are.

Secondly, ask a trusted colleague to give you five minutes of their time. Ask them to choose a particular geographical feature, landmark or building they know well. Then ask them to list as many different ways as they can in which the item may be 'appreciated or understood'. Give them an example to start them off (for example, St Paul's Cathedral in London may be understood as a religious building *or* in relation to Wren the architect, or aesthetically, and so on). Whilst they are compiling their list, construct your own. How similar were the two sets of suggestions?

continued

Alternatively, ask the colleague to think of three or more possible explanations for a simple scenario such as 'a man runs out of the post office looking distressed'.

Thirdly, imagine you are marking a piece of written work, the quality of which is some way above what you expected a particular student to produce. You want to end your written feedback with a positive comment. How many appropriate phrases can you think of in three minutes?

Finally, think of a problem you know about that arose in teaching (or in the organisation of teaching and learning) in the setting where you work in recent times. How was it resolved? Do you think it could have been resolved more *creatively*? If so, reflect on the meaning of 'creatively' in your answer.

A general approach

One of the best general introductions to the topic of creativity that is psychologically well-informed but also has a broad relevance and appeal is that written by Kneller (1965). Kneller's book provides a number of useful approaches to defining creativity, including a helpful categorisation of the four ways in which the term most often appears. Briefly, creativity may refer to: characteristics of a person who creates; a particular type of mental process; something that is related to environmental and cultural circumstances; or the outcomes, ideas or artefacts of a creative process. All four of these meanings feature in the literature on creativity.

For our purposes the most useful starting-point is Kneller's argument that creativity is always characterised by two things, namely *novelty* and *relevance*. The first of these refers to the arrival of something that is new or original, though this is usually a question of rearranging what is already known or done, so that we see a new relationship between things we have seen as separate in the past. The second characteristic, *relevance*, reminds us that creativity is always in a context, and Kneller argues that a creative act is a response to a situation in which something requires a solution or at least clarification. Indeed, a creative act only makes sense in relation to a particular situation.

But what happens in the creative process? Kneller offers us a version of an account of creativity which gained some popularity in the late 1950s and early 1960s and which describes creativity as a series of up to five stages. The first of these he calls *first insight*, which is the point at which we become aware that there is a problem to be solved or a difficulty to be overcome. This is followed by a period of *preparation*. Here the person 'reads, notes, discusses, questions, collects, explores' in relation to the problem. Contact with the ideas of others is particularly important, especially for the purposes of 'feeding imagination' or to 'fire ambition'. Exposing oneself to what others have managed to do well, or to the ways in which they were unsuccessful, can make us face up to (rather than avoid) difficulties. However, the ideas of others must also be set aside at some point if our own are to gain full expression.

Preparation is followed by a third stage called *incubation*, where the work is assumed to go underground, as it were, into a period of 'non-conscious activity'. This may last minutes or years, but results in the inspiration that leads to an original act. Kneller illustrates this with examples from mathematics and painting, though does not enter into detailed discussion about the nature of the unconscious processes themselves. Next comes *illumination*, the moment at which we grasp the concept or idea which makes all the others fall into place. Often sudden and unexpected, the moment of illumination has been commented upon time and again by a wide variety of artists and scientists. Some have remarked on the certainty they felt about having found the solution to a problem, even though it was yet to be verified: others have commented on the joy they felt when illumination occurred.

Finally, we enter a stage of *verification*, which can also incorporate revision. This is where 'intellect and judgement must complete the work that imagination has begun' especially as '. . . illumination is notoriously unreliable' (Kneller, p. 56). There is a standing back from the work, probably some emotional disengagement from it, and in many cases the seeking out of feedback from others. This stage, which may take a very long time in the case of major theoretical work, completes the process of creativity in this model.

Although he shares something of a classical psychological concern to distinguish between 'creative' and 'normal' people, Kneller also holds the view that a great deal of what goes on in educational establishments actually hinders rather than helps the nurturing of creative potential in *all* individuals. Indeed, a chapter on education completes Kneller's book. Having identified a list of the traits of creative people (which include such things as intelligence, awareness, fluency, scepticism and flexibility, and even humour and

Reflection

Kneller had the experiences of American college students in mind when he produced the ideas listed here. Look at the list again, then try to answer the following questions:

- To what extent do the items describe aspects of your own schooling?
- To what extent do you think they describe schooling for young people nowadays?
- To what extent do they describe the situation in which *teachers* find themselves?

non-conformity), Kneller talks of features of educational institutions that inhibit creativity. These include the following:

- an undervaluing of imagination;
- a heavy reliance on textbooks;
- social distance between teachers and learners;
- an over-emphasis on distinctive genders and roles;
- over-emphasis on the rewarding of accuracy in the reproduction of existing knowledge;
- the encouragement to make choices in the curriculum and assessment which are 'safe' in that they minimise risk-taking and maximise credentials. (adapted from Kneller, 1965, p. 76).

Kneller's discussion of the education system begins to acknowledge that creativity is something for everyone – or at least all learners. He prefers an integrated approach to the problem of increasing the attention that is given to creativity in the curriculum. His approach is all about training the mind to think creatively as well as logically. It includes the promotion of originality (for example encouraging students to evaluate or produce their own versions of events in a way that gives explicit reward to originality), whilst at the same time realising that different occasions call for different levels of originality. Secondly, it includes 'sustain[ing] the student's delight in novelty' (p. 80). This includes a deliberate promotion of the idea that knowledge is constructed, so that the teacher '. . . should emphasize that the more we discover the more we realize how incomplete our knowledge is' (p. 81), and making sure that students who ask interesting questions, which may well sound fanciful to the rest of the class, are congratulated for doing so. Furthermore, the teacher should encourage a range of associated habits and skills including inventiveness (for example by using 'brainstorming', where students have a chance to produce many potential solutions to a problem before any is subjected to a critical evaluation of worth) and 'fluency' with the articulation of concepts. Teachers should challenge their students with provocative ideas but also find ways in which to increase the students' confidence in those they develop themselves. A certain amount of contact with the words and deeds of past creative thinkers can be helpful, provided it is not enough to make the student feel that their own efforts are worthless by comparison. Lastly, the teacher has a role in nurturing in students qualities such as: a sensitivity to problems; curiosity and a desire to enquire; independent study; powers of observation and perception; and ability to make connections between previously unconnected ideas.

Kneller's ultimate concern is with the promotion of creativity in learners, in the sense that the teacher or wider educational establishment can do much to foster in most (or perhaps all) learners the capacity to engage in the five stages he identified as summarising the creative process. Of more immediate interest is whether or not the model he presents applies to teachers and the ways in which they may be more or less creative. The people that educate the teacher and those that manage the teacher and the circumstances within which he or she works can all make a real difference here. Management issues form part of the discussion in Chapter 8.

The act of creation

A particularly compelling notion of creativity is to be found in the work of Arthur Koestler, a British author born in 1905 in Hungary, who is well-known for both his novels and his non-fictional writing, including political commentary. In one of his later books (*The Act of Creation*, first published in 1964) Koestler constructed a fascinating theory which went some way in explaining all manner of creative acts of people, and in particular, the features these have in common. He demonstrated that, contrary to most expectations, the origins of major creative acts in humour, in science and in art were rather similar, without clear boundaries between them. The way in which they really differed from one another was to do with the conditions prevailing in each case. To reflect this idea, the book is divided into three parts, entitled 'The jester', 'The sage' and 'The artist', each one packed with detailed discussion and examples. There is only the space here to give the briefest of introductions to the ideas presented in such a large work. However, it is possible to indicate the essence of the approach with sufficient clarity to begin to explore its relevance to the work of the teacher.

A good starting-point is the idea that we tend to put 'thinking' on a pedestal and forget that most of it is a practical, everyday business. Koestler insists that most of the thinking we do is, in important respects, like riding a bicycle:

> ❝ . . . *there is less difference between the routines of thinking and bicycle-riding than our self-esteem would make us believe. Both are governed by implicit codes of which we are only dimly aware, and which we are unable to specify.*
> (Koestler, 1969, p. 44)

But Koestler distinguishes between these everyday routines and *creative* thinking, so how does he describe creativity? At one level the answer is quite simple. He proposes that all acts of creativity depend upon an association between two otherwise separate contexts (he calls this a 'bisociation'). Jokes are a common form of creativity, and they provide a good illustration of the basic idea. Here is an example he uses himself:

 Two women meet while shopping at the supermarket in the Bronx. One looks cheerful, the other looks depressed. The cheerful one inquires:
'What's eating you?'
'Nothing's eating me.'
'Death in the family?'
'No, God forbid!'
'Worried about money?'
'No . . . nothing like that.'
'Trouble with the kids?'
'Well, if you must know, it's my little Jimmy.'
'What's wrong with him, then?'
'Nothing is wrong. His teacher said he must see a psychiatrist.'
Pause. 'Well, what's wrong with seeing a psychiatrist?'
'Nothing is wrong. The psychiatrist said he's got an Oedipus complex.'
Pause. 'Well, well, Oedipus or Schmoedipus, I wouldn't worry so long as he's a good boy and loves his mamma.'   (Koestler, 1969, pp. 32–3)

Like many jokes, this one produces a clash between two completely different frames of reference. On the one hand, there is the common-sense frame of reference, within which we might agree that if little Jimmy is good and loves his mother there can't be much that is wrong. However, a second frame of reference is introduced, namely a particular Freudian interpretation of the relationship between the boy and his mother. For all its simplicity, the story resonates on two mutually incompatible levels at one and the same time, and this is probably the main reason it makes some people laugh. Koestler argues that this effect of bisociation is fundamental in the creation of humour.

If we accept that this is the process at work with (at least some forms of) humour, how does the idea of bisociation apply to the gaining of new knowledge in science and art? Koestler begins his exploration of scientific creativity with an account of some famous investigative work with chimpanzees from early this century which provides convincing evidence that primates can experience 'insightful learning' and solve certain kinds of problems. However, he is not at this point describing the creativity of the scientist so much as that of the chimpanzees themselves. Their discovery that a stick may be used to reach a banana necessitates the putting together of two very familiar things – sticks and reaching for food – in new ways. From here he moves on to Archimedes, whose cry of 'Eureka!' followed perhaps the most celebrated example of insightful learning in history. Archimedes had the difficulty of assessing the purity of a golden crown without the luxury of melting it down. He knew how heavy a given volume of gold should be, but had no way of measuring the volume of the crown with any accuracy. Until, that is, he lowered himself into the bath and saw (in a new light) the water level rising by an amount that would equal the volume of his own body. Once more, bisociation seems to be at work. Archimedes' creative act was to connect two hitherto unconnected frames of reference. The point is not that either of them was on its own particularly original or imaginative – we can appreciate that both the weighing of gold and the taking of baths could be fairly routine in the circumstances – but that a problem was solved by bringing the two together.

Koestler goes on to provide other case studies of scientific discovery, including the work of Pasteur on vaccination; that of mathematicians such as Ampere and Gauss; and in some greater detail, the work of Gutenberg, Kepler and Darwin. With each, his main point is that creativity is defined by the stepping outside of one way of working, the re-combination of old ideas into new forms, and 'the uncovering of what was always there':

> *This leads to the paradox that the more original a discovery the more obvious it seems afterwards. The creative act is not an act of creation in the sense of the Old Testament. It does not create something out of nothing; it uncovers, selects, re-shuffles, combines, synthesizes already existing facts, ideas, faculties, skills. The more familiar the parts, the more striking the new whole.* (Koestler, 1969, p. 120)

Turning to artistic production, Koestler argues that much the same process is at work. Where the scientist sees an analogy, the poet discovers an original metaphor or simile: both rely on the putting together of two normally disconnected frames of reference. In a discussion of what he calls 'illusion', Koestler shows how the successful *reception* of an artistic process also depends on a form of bisociation. We may watch a play or film which affects us deeply, yet all the while we know that it is 'really' a group of actors with a script, or some patterns of light projected on to a screen. The fact that this effect is commonplace does not make it any the less remarkable, and Koestler is convincing in his attempt to demonstrate just how important is this 'capacity for living in two universes at once, one real, one imaginary' (ibid. p. 302).

Although it shares with other approaches a justifiable fascination with the creativity of the most celebrated scientists, artists and others, Koestler's ideas about the way in which creativity comes about are inherently accessible and offer us plenty to think about in educational contexts. For example, the compartmentalisation of the curriculum into subjects has undoubted advantages, yet we might ask ourselves whether our learners have sufficient opportunities to work on the boundaries between subjects or on problems which require a multi-disciplinary approach. Are we giving our learners the mistaken impression that in the wider world there are such things as problems that are *purely* geographical, chemical, financial or mathematical? How do we deal with the paradox that a good teacher of subject x might be a teacher who manages to bring in subjects a, b, c and d?

These are important considerations, though perhaps the most interesting avenue to pursue is the way we maintain and enhance our own subject knowledge for the purposes of teaching. Surely, we are more likely to be enthusiastic about the teaching of our subject if we ourselves discover new meanings, applications and resonances that we can communicate to our students? This is not to say that the teacher of statistics has to be a great innovator in the history of the subject (this is not only unrealistic but for most teaching situations would probably be a disadvantage). But it is to say that the teacher of statistics who gets the class to help her to construct an amusing, annotated cartoon drawing of a double-decker bus to illustrate the different uses of numbers (*nominal* for the route number on the front, *ordinal* for shoe sizes of passengers, *interval* for their IQ scores and *ratio* for the speedometer, and so on) is doing much more than providing a quirky *aide mémoire*: she is engaging in a creative act which is likely to encourage further creative acts on the part of students. Likewise, the science teacher who often steps outside the prescribed list of learning outcomes to get students to assess the ethical, social, medical or economic dimensions of physical or chemical processes is also engaging in a form of creativity. In each of these cases the teacher's preparation is likely to include some reformulation of their own knowledge, for which they need to be open to new sources of information and new ways of seeing familiar territory. Part of their lesson preparation might take the form of finding settings and situations outside the immediate subject matter that will connect in interesting ways with it. This in turn requires a teacher who is willing to acknowledge that schools and colleges are not the only places in which people learn things. Once with their students, they are in turn effectively sharing their own recent creativity. Koestler's *bisociation* seems to be a useful thinking tool if we wish to get beyond simplistic notions of knowledge transmission.

Critical thinking

The book by Kneller referred to earlier in the chapter was motivated in part by a desire to see more creativity nurtured in the (North American) education system. Kneller sees this as a desirable goal because for him 'to be creative is to fulfil oneself as a person'. This goal is very close to that in a related set of ideas developed in the adult education literature by Stephen Brookfield. Brookfield's interest is in the promotion of what he calls *critical thinking* in all walks of life, including education.

> *One important aspect of critical thinking is a kind of meta-thinking, or a capacity to see the circumstances in which one's thinking is taking place; however, it is also about knowledge of oneself and one's values and about being open to new ideas at every level. The critical thinker is sceptical about quick-fix solutions and about claims to universal truth. They are able to increase their autonomy, make more decisions for themsleves. As critical thinkers, . . . we become actively engaged in creating our personal and social worlds. In short, we take the reality of democracy seriously.* (Brookfield, 1987, p. x)

Brookfield's book *Developing Critical Thinkers* begins with an account of the various ways in which the notion of critical thinking featured in debate in the USA in the mid- to late 1980s. Rather like the idea of 'the learning society' in the UK and elsewhere in the 1990s, critical thinking has been seen as something of a panacea, as the key to increasing participation in civic and political life and even as a way in which to stimulate economic capacity in the face of new forms of foreign competition. Mostly, however, the term has been used to refer to such matters as logical reasoning, the making of judgments and reflecting on these, and the use and testing of meanings. Some writers have specified component traits, attributes or qualities such as flexibility, being sceptical, being honest, or being able to distinguish between facts and opinions, bias and reason.

Brookfield's own concept is a broader one which is not at all constrained by a concern with the cognitive, or the mechanics of thinking, or the capacity of individuals to search for empirical evidence to test particular assertions. It is closer to ideas like *emancipatory learning*, *dialectical thinking* and *reflective learning*. The first of these comes from the work of Jurgen Habermas (for example, Habermas, 1976) where it forms one of three 'domains' of learning, alongside *technical* and *communicative* learning. North Amercian adult educators have found this distinction very useful: *emancipatory learning* is the sort of learning that enables people to see the constraints in which they live in a new light and then act to change their circumstances for the better. The second term, *dialectical thinking*, refers to ways of looking at the world that in the words of one author, 'looks for, recognises, and welcomes contradictions as a stimulus to development' (Deshler, quoted in Brookfield, 1987, p. 13). Change is seen as a constant feature of life if we think dialectically. With the third related idea, Brookfield illustrates a reflective dimension to his own notion of critical thinking. Reflective learning refers to any process of careful examination of experiences to arrive at new understandings, and may be intellectual or affective (that is, to do with feelings), or indeed both.

In taking his argument forward, Brookfield continually reminds the reader that he is not just talking about critical thinking as a set of skills in an academic setting, but as something which is a normal part of everyday life. There are two activities, which are often observable though not always separated, namely *identifying and challenging assumptions* and *exploring and imagining alternatives*. These are illustrated in the following case study.

Case study

Andrew has taught French in a large secondary school for just over three years. This is his first post after qualifying. He is conscientious and works hard for his students, making a point of showing he values all progress and not just that of the academic high-fliers who, historically, have been the hallmark of the school.

However, increasingly, Andrew finds he is having difficulty with a number of students in two of the classes he teaches regularly. These students seem to spend longer and longer diverting lessons with (mostly spurious) requests and provocative comments, and there have been several very heated exchanges that have left Andrew feeling that he has let everyone down, especially the other students. He has followed the school's procedures to the letter, informing the head of year of the problems and suggesting that a number of parents/carers are informed that their sons and daughters are disrupting the learning of other students. Andrew has well-developed reflexive habits, though tends to blame himself rather easily when things go wrong. He feels he should not be 'losing his rag' so easily. He talks to some more experienced colleagues but does not find them of much help: one says that nothing can really be done because order is breaking down across the whole of society, whilst the other suggests that Andrew could experiment with making himself appear as more assertive.

One day soon after this, a student makes and repeats a racist remark at the beginning of the lesson. Andrew knows that the school has an explicit policy on this, so tells the student that the remark is unacceptable and refers the matter to the head of year. The same thing happens in the following lesson with the group. By the end of the week a meeting has been arranged with the head of year, the headteacher, the student's parents and Andrew himself. Andrew feels very uncomfortable during the meeting. As he expected, the student denied making repeated racist remarks, but it is only afterwards that he realises his discomfort was caused by the fact that during the meeting, his version of events was not being treated any more seriously than the student's. He feels let down by his managers and that the policy means little or nothing in practice.

Andrew decides to write down what is happening. This makes him more certain that something needs to change, and gives him the confidence to go and see the headteacher. In his meeting with the head, he explains patiently but firmly that in order to teach well, he needs the security of knowing where the boundaries of acceptable and unacceptable behaviour are drawn, and that his recent experience undermined rather than confirmed these boundaries both for him and for his students. Having thought it through, he tells the head that he is considering three options, namely (a) whether he should leave teaching; (b) whether he should try

Reflection

- To what extent does Andrew's story illustrate Brookfield's idea that critical thinking involves *identifying and challenging assumptions* and *exploring and imagining alternatives*?
- What sorts of *risks* does Andrew take in the case study?
- Are there similarities and differences between Andrew's strategy and courses of action you have taken yourself?

to move to a new job in a different school, or (c) whether he should try to get colleagues involved in discussions so as to produce some recommendations about school policies and procedures for the Senior Management Team to consider. The headteacher, knowing Andrew is a good teacher and therefore an asset to the school, encourages him to take the third option.

Clearly, 'identifying and challenging assumptions' does not mean the same thing as an automatic (and probably quite annoying) questioning of everything all the time. Nor does it imply that we just look out for what others are doing wrongly or badly. What it does mean is the subjecting to scrutiny of our own and other people's 'habitual ways of thinking and acting', with a view to finding how we – as well as they – might change things. This requires a good awareness of context, of the ways in which social and cultural factors permit or deny certain assumptions, and Brookfield is surely quite right to suggest that it can be quite threatening to our sense of self when we discover that so much of what we took to be personal behavioural property is in another sense socially ordained. There are several similarities here with the idea of *habitus* as developed by the French social theorist Pierre Bourdieu (see for example Grenfell and James, 1998).

The second activity, namely exploring and imagining alternatives, must begin with some realisation that alternatives are 'thinkable', or can exist. Again this is potentially highly threatening and destabilising, but it can also be liberating. It seems particularly relevant to teachers, because they often deal directly with forms of knowledge. They can:

 ... become suspicious of those who tell us that they have 'the answer' to life or the solution to all our problems. In short we develop reflective skepticism; we do not take for granted the universal truth of some statement, policy, or justification simply because of the authority ascribed to the source of this supposed truth ... Reflective skepticism is present whenever individuals call into question the belief that simply because some idea or social structure has existed unchanged for a period of time, it therefore must be (a) right and (b) the best possible arrangement.
(Brookfield, 1987, p. 21)

Brookfield is at pains to point out that none of this means adopting a purely 'relativist' stance, in which nothing is held as a genuine belief, and everything is taken to be temporary or provisional. We can and probably should be committed to particular ideas, people and causes, and our commitment is likely to be all the more solid for having been subjected to critical scrutiny which involves a thorough comparison with our experiences and/or those we know about.

Brookfield comes at the processes of critical thinking from a number of different angles, one of which is to suggest that it is understandable as a process with characteristic phases or stages. Here the parallels with the steps in creativity are really quite striking. For Brookfield, people often begin to think critically when they see what they take to be an anomaly or 'contradiction between how the world is supposed to work . . . and their own experiences of reality' (p. 24). This phase Brookfield calls a *trigger event*, and it is usually a major 'turning point' which gives rise to discomfort, dissonance or confusion. This is very similar to Kneller's *first insight* stage. It is followed by *appraisal*, where there is self-scrutiny and a general clarification of the problem or concern and often a connecting with others in a similar situation. Thirdly, a stage of *exploration* takes us into a search for new explanations or actions which hold out the possibility of reducing the discomfort we feel. We may try new roles and even identities. This is followed by *developing alternative perspectives* and then *integration*, stages in which we achieve a transition to a new settlement as the end result of a process of change that we recognise as learning. The elements of these stages have much in common with the stage Kneller called *preparation*. But whilst critical thinking is on the whole described as more of a conscious and deliberate process than creativity, there is often a non-conscious component here too, as there was in Kneller's *incubation* stage. Brookfield quotes Boyd and Fales for whom integration '. . . appears to represent an unconscious selection of previously assimilated information, which emerges in consciousness as a full formulated integration' (Boyd and Fales, 1983, p. 110). In a further parallel, the individual who becomes aware of this integration may well feel genuine satisfaction and even elation.

There are three other important ways in which critical thinking and some concepts of creativity come together. Firstly, both refer to activities that are well within the capabilities of most people – indeed most people engage in the activities most of the time. Secondly, both aim to provide us with ideas for educating in particular ways so as to *develop* habits and capacities that will be genuinely useful to people. Thirdly, these ideas come from a careful consideration of evidence derived from first-hand or reported experiences.

A professional notion of creativity

The discussion above shows that there are a number of overlapping concepts of creativity which may have real implications for teaching. One of the justifications for presenting these is that different elements of them are likely to be of interest to different teachers. However, it could be argued that some ideas are more generally helpful than others when we consider this range of meanings.

This point is argued well in an article published in a collection originally aimed at teacher educators (Halliwell, 1993), where it is suggested that the most important notions of creativity for teachers are those that might 'stimulate and enhance learning' (p. 69). For Halliwell, this means that: (a) we are not focusing on 'creativity as genius' because we are concerned with the unique requirements of ordinary situations rather than extraordinary ones; (b) we are not primarily concerned with the idea of teachers themselves becoming so creative that they 'dazzle' learners with their performances; (c) we are not talking about the capacity of teachers to develop their artistic or aesthetic capacities, however valuable this may be in its own right. Rather, creative teachers need to be *inventive* and *responsive*. Halliwell suggests that this depends on arriving at:

- a clear sense of need;
- the ability to read the situation;
- the willingness to take risks;
- the ability to monitor and evaluate events.   (ibid. p. 71)

She goes on to suggest a number of ways in which teacher educators can contribute towards developing these capacities, all the while ensuring that there is adequate 'ownership', described by Woods (1990) as an essential part of creativity. Her main concern is with what happens in teacher education (and especially in the light of a move to a greater proportion of training being school-based) but most of her final recommendations can be used as a checklist by more established teachers who wish to see what opportunities they might have to enhance their own 'responsive inventiveness'. Teachers might ask themselves:

- Do I have plenty of opportunities to share experiences as they happen, not just talk about them afterwards with someone who, however interested, was not there?
- Do I engage in extensive collaborative work?
- Is there the climate and opportunity for constructive peer criticism?
- Is my performance judged in ways that go beyond narrow indicators?
- Are there opportunities for me to step out of my responsibilities from time to time to become a true learner in relation to my work?

(adapted from Halliwell, 1993, p. 78)

Creativity is a theoretical construct that, as we have seen, has a range of meanings. However, several of these meanings would seem to have something important to say to teachers. Creativity draws attention to the practical side of teaching and its development, and some of the ways in which teachers might learn through reflective practice. It follows that being a creative professional involves such activities as isolating, articulating, examining and resolving (whether completely or in part) the problems that arise in one's practice as an educator. This may be thought of as an 'everyday' form of action research, an approach which has much to offer the teacher who can begin to examine their work and situation in terms of the degree of harmony or discord between their values and practices (see for example Whitehead, 1993; McNiff, 1993).

Professional creativity should not be taken as suggesting some sort of runaway experimentation with what we and our students do together. Rather, it asserts that responsible experimentation and innovation, planned and monitored with the help of colleagues as well as relevant theoretical notions, are desirable activities. Furthermore, they are the proper concern of the professional teacher who wishes to keep open the door to improvement of their practice.

References

ASHWORTH, M. (1998) 'Interpretations of creativity: the diversity of teachers' views and implications for the promotion of creativity across the curriculum'. Paper presented at the *British Educational Research Association Conference*, Queen's University Belfast.

BEETLESTONE, F. (1998) *Creative Children, Imaginative Teaching*, Buckingham: Open University Press.

BOYD, E. M., and FAYLES, A. W. (1983) 'Reflective learning: key to learning from experience', *Journal of Humanistic Psychology*, **23**, 2, pp. 99–117.

BROOKFIELD, S. D. (1987) *Developing Critical Thinkers – Challenging Adults to Explore Alternative Ways of Thinking and Acting*, Buckingham: Open University Press.

FRYER, M. (1996) *Creative Teaching and Learning*, London: Paul Chapman Publishing.

GALTON, F. (1884) *Hereditary Genius*, New York: D. Appleton.

GOULD, S. J. (1981) *The Mismeasure of Man*, London: Penguin.

GRENFELL, M. and JAMES, D. (1998) *Bourdieu and Education: Acts of Practical Theory*, London: Falmer Press.

GUILFORD, J. P. (1957) 'Creative abilities in the arts', *Psychological Review*, **64**, pp. 110–18.

HABERMAS, J. (1976) *Communication and the Evolution of Society*, London: Routledge.

HALLIWELL, S. (1993) 'Teacher creativity and teacher education', in BRIDGES, D. and KERRY, T. (eds) *Developing Teachers Professionally: Reflections for Initial and In-service Trainers*, London: Routledge.

KNELLER, G. F. (1965) *The Art and Science of Creativity*, New York: Holt, Rinehart and Winston.

KOESTLER, A. (1969) *The Act of Creation* (Danube Edition), London: Hutchinson and Co.

McNIFF, J. (1993) *Teaching as Learning*, London: Routledge.

VERNON, P. E. (1970) *Creativity*, Harmondsworth: Penguin.

WHITEHEAD, J. (1993) *The Growth of Educational Knowledge*, Bournemouth: Hyde Publications.

WOODS, P. (1990) *Teacher Skills and Strategies*, Lewes: Falmer Press.

Further reading

As will be clear from the discussion in this chapter, Koestler's *The Act of Creation* (reference above) is a fascinating read for several different reasons, and is particularly good if you already have an interest in the history of science. Brookfield's *Developing Critical Thinkers* (reference above) is well worth reading if you feel that you would like to explore new and potentially 'empowering' ways of thinking about your work and work situation. The closely related writing of action researchers may also be of particular interest: Jean McNiff's *Action Research: Principles and Practice* (1988, London: Macmillan) and her *Teaching as Learning* (reference above) provide helpful structures in a very accessible style.

Chapter 3

Creative teaching and reflective practice
Keith Postlethwaite

Why be creative?

 Do what you've always done and you'll get what you always got!

For teachers, this common business management axiom can be reassuring. It implies that our tried and trusted methods of teaching can be relied upon to produce the kinds of outcomes that we have come to expect for our students. However, this apparent reassurance can mask a problem. We may want to improve on these reliable outcomes, or we may want to continue to deliver them despite some new constraint such as a changed legal framework, or reduced resources, or larger class sizes. We may want to make these outcomes attainable by a wider range of individuals, such as students with difficulty in basic skills. We may want to enable students from a wider range of cultural backgrounds to attain what, previously, a narrower student group had been able to do. If so, then we have to do something new. We have to adopt a creative approach to our teaching.

We also need to be creative for a more subtle reason. Teaching is not a matter of routine application of a technique in a well-defined and well-controlled context. Every class is different because of its different history and the complexity of its inter-personal dynamics. Individual learners are different because of their social and psychological characteristics, their cognitive strengths and weaknesses, and the nature of their formal and informal prior learning. Every time with a given class or given learner is different because of the complex interplay of events that can lead to temporary, or even permanent, changes in any of the factors mentioned above. To respond to this flux with familiar classes and with familiar learners, we constantly need to be creative – even if our goals are not new; even if our context has not changed.

Reflective practice as a framework for creativity

Yet even if we recognise a need for creativity, the nature of teaching can appear to prevent it. Our working day, with its hundreds of interactions with individuals, its endless flow of short-term deadlines, its constant stream of administrative demands and the odd intrusion of the totally unexpected, is hardly designed to help us create new ways of thinking and acting. Fortunately, there are helpful structures which can support our search for creativity. I should like to concentrate on one: reflective practice. It can certainly be caricatured: for some, reflective practice means little more than pausing to wonder whether a lesson 'went well' or 'went badly'. However, taken seriously and in its fuller meaning, reflective practice can provide us with powerful tools for advancing what we do in education, and our thinking about that enterprise.

A key person in the development of the notion of reflective practice is Donald Schön (1983). He urges that, 'to create the knowledge which is of value to (us) in informing action' we should reflect on the *implicit understandings* which have guided our actions to date and 'criticise, restructure and re-apply that understanding'.

This is crucial because it links our actions (as we re-apply our understanding) to our thinking, to that understanding itself. It therefore calls for creativity with respect to ideas as well as creativity with respect to action. Indeed, without the former, the latter is impossible for our range for action will be limited by the limitations inherent in our old ideas.

In talking about our thinking, Schön puts our own personal and often implicit theories about teaching and learning in the centre of the picture. These are theories we have constructed to make sense of our experience as teachers and learners. As an example, it may be that, over time, we have come to a generalised personal view that, on a windy day, the students are always 'high' and that a less active lesson style then tends to be more effective. But what is the status of these theories, how valid are they? Certainly they stand the test of our own personal day-to-day use, otherwise they would not survive in our own thinking. However, this does not ensure that they are entirely valid – even for us. Firstly, our experiences, through which we test out our theories, will be limited. We may work mainly with poorly motivated students, so our theory about the windy day, generated in this context, may lead us astray when we apply it elsewhere in our teaching. Secondly, our observation of our own practice may be coloured by our theories, so we tend to go on seeing what our theories lead us to expect, even though the reality of our classroom may be somewhat different. There may have been one or two very powerful experiences of 'high' students on windy days and these override the observation that others might make that on most other windy days, our students are no different from normal. We, however, impressed by the vividness of the memories, fail to notice this and therefore fail to modify our theory. Also, the basis of our observation may be limited: for example we may notice that less active learning styles lead to a more controlled class on windy days, but may fail to observe the impact on other aspects of the quality of the students' learning.

If we are going to be creative about the development of our teaching, we need therefore to do just as Schön suggests and subject these theories to critical analysis, so that we are no longer trapped by theories that, once we have thought about them in an explicit way, we recognise as needing to be developed or even rejected. The immediate question is, 'How can I identify my personal, implicit theories?'

Identifying personal theories

Since no one can tackle all aspects of their educational thinking and practice at once, it is important to focus on something that is becoming problematic for you, perhaps for one of the reasons outlined at the beginning of this chapter. Then in relation to this aspect of teaching, have a trusted colleague observe your teaching and talk to you about things related to that aspect of teaching that *they felt you did well* – what you actually did; how you achieved those things; why you did what you did. Focusing on successful aspects of your teaching helps you to avoid justificatory explanations of your actions and encourages you to bring to the surface the principles which guided you. Amongst these will be your personal theories of teaching and learning.

Once you have discussed the positive things in this aspect of your teaching, you may feel able to raise more problematic things with your colleague and talk about the basis of these actions too. This, however, can be under your control: you do as much or as little as you wish.

What is interesting here is that your colleague's description of your actions may surprise you. It is tempting to dismiss their account, especially where it is about things of which you are not very proud. However, this would be unwise. It can be very difficult for anyone to form a fully rounded view of their own classroom practice. When we try to map our practice, we are all coloured by our intentions as well as our actions, and tend to concentrate on the unusual or the dramatic aspects, perhaps involving one or two students, ignoring the general experience for the class as a whole. Colleagues' views can therefore bring new information for your consideration, perhaps triggering the discussion of more problematic aspects of practice as indicated above and therefore extending the range of personal theories to which you acquire access.

The colleague in question does not have to be a more experienced teacher. You may find yourself working alongside student teachers as well as more experienced colleagues: student teachers can be very good at asking about aspects of your teaching. As well as helping the students themselves to learn to teach, discussion of these matters can give *you* the kinds of insights we are seeking in this section. If student teachers are well-prepared for the task, they will understand the need to focus on positive aspects of your teaching – if not, you may have to help them understand the reasons for doing so.

Video recording and audio recording of lessons, and requests to your own students for their feedback, can be other useful sources of insight into your actions, stimulating further discussion with a colleague of the background to this action. However, if you ask your students, you must be willing to accept what they say without getting angry or defensive. (You might explicitly plan how you could do this, before launching the request.) If students once feel that they were asked for their views and, having given them honestly, were subjected to the teacher's anger, or to less favourable treatment in class, trust will be lost and may take a very long time to re-establish. This is not to say that you have to take their description of your teaching as the only one which counts, but you do have to take it as honest expression of their *perception* of that teaching – a perception that will undoubtedly influence their response whatever its actual basis in fact. Insight into this perception can therefore be enormously valuable to you, and you need to let students know that you treat it as such, even if (perhaps especially if) you disagree strongly with what they are saying.

Significant teachers from your own past as a learner will certainly have had a strong influence on your personal theories of teaching and learning. For example, you are likely to set up a personal theory that a particular approach to, say, the management of practical work is useful, if it was one used by a teacher you admired. It may therefore be useful to explore an extra way of getting insights into what you have learned from your 'observation through experience' of the teachers who have been significant for you. One possible method, based on aspects of personal construct theory (Fransella and Bannister, 1977; Kelly, 1955), is described below.

First you need to list individual teachers from your past, including those whom you felt were particularly influential. They need not all be from the same educational context – you might include primary, secondary and further or higher education teachers, and within any one phase, teachers from any of the schools or colleges you attended. Then form several groups of three teachers, by random selection of individuals from your list. (Ten to fifteen groups is likely to be sufficient.) Writing individual teachers' names on pieces of card can be helpful in achieving this goal as three cards can be selected at random from the pack, the names noted, then the cards returned to the pack before the process is repeated. A given teacher can occur in more than one group of three, though try not to have two teachers the same in consecutive groups. Then for each group of teachers in turn, decide how to split it into a pair and a single so that the teachers in the pair have something in common, and are different from the teacher who is the single. Then ask yourself what the pair have in common, and how the single is different.

> For example, Mr A, Ms B and Ms C form a group of three.
> Mr A and Ms C are the pair; Ms B the single, because
> Mr A and Ms C give students choice; Ms B directs all aspects of the lesson herself

This 'construct' (student choice . . . teacher-direction) is then identified as something that you have learned about teaching from your own experiences as a learner. Other constructs will emerge from the process, until at some point you will begin to find them being repeated.

Already, it is clear that a list of personal constructs could help you to make new connections. In relation to the example above, it might transpire that the descriptions of your practice indicate that you tend to be very directive: you may begin to see that this is, at least in part, because Ms B really impressed you and you are (possibly implicitly) modelling her practice in your own teaching.

One useful extension of this process is to include yourself in the list of teachers and see if new insights are generated when you are one of the three teachers under consideration in a group of three. Another extension is to list all of the constructs (for example including student choice . . . teacher-direction); set up a scale of 1–5 with 1 being identified with one end (pole) of each construct and 5 with the other. (For the construct in the example above, 1 might be taken to mean 'giving students choice'; 5 might be taken to mean 'teacher-directed'.) Then give yourself a score on each of the constructs. The pattern of scores can give you an interesting insight into how *you see yourself* as a teacher in terms of the range of ideas that you have generated from your experience of the teacher who taught you.

Discussions of things you do well, discussions (on your terms) of things that are problematic for you, and the personal construct activity outlined above, will all lead to a more explicit understanding of your personal theories. These are very important, perhaps for the very reason that they are personal – we construct them from our own experience and use them to structure our own actions. However, they may not be the only influence on what you do, so it may be useful to look at other influences on your practice.

Identifying other grounds for your practice

To gain different insights into other aspects of the basis of your actions, it is useful to *analyse* more thoroughly the actions that you have taken. The key question at this point is, 'Why, apart from in response to my personal theories, did I do X?'

It may be that you did something because some piece of educational theory or research paper which you have studied in the past (*formal theory*), suggested that it would be appropriate, and you have taken this on board as part of your framework for action. It may be that:

■ you did something because a favourite teacher from your past as a student, or a much respected colleague, did it that way and again, this approach has become part of *your* approach;

■ you were exploiting some specific opportunity like access to a lecture theatre, or the fact that the students had recently been on a relevant school trip;

■ you were responding to some constraint such as a lack of resources, or the fact that the furniture in the room limited the style of the lesson in some way;

■ you were following school policy or responding to your understanding of parental expectations, or to an understanding of the recent history of your school (for example the outcome of a recent inspection, or the consequences of a move into a new building).

These influences are all examples of the impact of *local context* on decision making. Constraints imposed by law (for example in the content of a science class on sex), or by the values which are common or the subject of current debate in society (*national context*) may have affected you. You may have acted as you did because of some deeply held belief or principle about young people and the way they learn, for example that students ought to have a say in decisions made about their education (*your own values*).

The Enquiry task which follows should help you in structuring this kind of analysis.

Enquiry task: Analysing actions as a spur to change

For all of the ideas below, again focus on one aspect of your teaching with one class – for example, working with the most able students in that class, your use of questioning with a given group, marking homework, working with groups. Keep the same aspect of teaching in mind as you work through each of the sections.

Formal theories:
Identify the range of relevant theories
- With the given aspect of teaching in mind, work with a group of colleagues to brainstorm the relevant 'big ideas'. These might come from the group's experiences of reading, of continuing professional development (CPD) courses, of initial teacher education (ITE) courses. Start to construct a list of the theories.
- You might also talk about relevant theories to colleagues involved in teacher education (lecturers in a university education faculty; colleagues in school involved as mentors in ITE courses; professional tutors in school; student teachers in the later stages of their course) and again list the relevant 'big ideas'.
- Another possible source of insight is the Contents pages of books about education.

Then highlight theories which you think influenced you
- On your own, go through the list highlighting anything that had an influence on your actions in relation to the aspect of teaching which you are considering.

Context:
Perhaps through talk with others, *list the* opportunities *and the* constraints *that surround the particular aspect of teaching and learning with which you are concerned.* To do this, think about the specific class and make a list including:
- the resources available – books, equipment, non-teaching staff, ICT etc;
- physical features of the room – size, furniture, neighbours, suitability for use of AV equipment etc;
- timetable issues – when in the day does this teaching happen, which day, what have the students done before?;
- the characteristics of the students – for example, ability, motivation, formal and informal learning to date, preferred learning style, preferred mode of gaining information (aural, visual, action-based), preferred mode of recording information (oral, written, making something), inter-personal dynamics in the class (who gets on with whom, or not);
- the expectations of the school and department or college (as in policy statements and handbooks and as evident from the folklore of the place, and so on);
- the expectations of parents;
- recent history of the class (and the school or college more generally);
- national context (such as, requirements of National Curriculum, syllabus constraints, legal aspects – for example with issues such as sex education or with safety in laboratories, workshops. art rooms, gymnasia etc).

Then highlight the factors which you think influenced you
- On your own, go through the above list highlighting anything that had an influence on your actions in relation to the aspect of teaching which you are considering.

Your values:
Identify the range of your personal values
With the specific aspect of teaching in mind try to complete the following sentences:
- Students should/ought…
- Teachers should/ought…
- It is important that…

Such sentences, when complete, tend to reveal key values which you will have in mind (at least in the back of your mind) when you are making decisions.

Then highlight factors that you think especially influenced you
- Go through the sentences you have written highlighting anything that had an influence on your actions in relation to the aspect of teaching that you are considering.

Evaluation

What we have done so far is to explore ways in which we can look at the reasons behind the actions we take in our teaching. Another component in the analysis of our actions, is whether or not, and in what ways, these actions were successful – we need to *evaluate* our actions. The key question now is, 'Was it appropriate to take that specific action?'

Evaluations of a specific action are important and can lead to decisions to change how we do certain things. However, *many* of our actions will be influenced by our personal theories, so another level of evaluation is, 'Is this personal theory appropriate?' Because personal theories have widespread relevance to our teaching, answers to this question can have a widespread effect on the development of that teaching.

Gathering data

At one level, we usually have a 'feel' for the effectiveness of our actions once a lesson ends. But we need to be careful. These impressions can be based on very selective information. One difficult moment can convince us that the lesson was awful, whereas for most of the time and for most of the learners it was good. Also, it is important to recognise that impressions (and some more formal evaluations) can be based on a very limited set of criteria. Beginning teachers are often dominated by concerns about survival: it was a good lesson if they came out of the class with all the students they started with and with no significant riots! As they become more experienced, beginning teachers can also take account of how well they put over the content and processes that they had prepared. A more experienced teacher would, in addition, ask about the quality of learning. An expert teacher might also judge whether she was successful in maintaining a policy of equal opportunities, or in extending the most able as well as supporting the least able, or in developing the self-confidence as well as the conceptual understanding of her students.

These impressions, then, may give some information about the effects of what you did, but they need to be refined. You may need to find out more clearly what the consequences of your actions were. This involves taking a broad enough view. You will want information on students' understanding of the *content* of the lesson – did they learn the lesson content that we intended them to learn; were there any unexpected learning outcomes (for example additional insights into the topic, or misconceptions); at what level was the learning (for example did students learn facts or did they analyse an argument)? Bloom's *Taxonomy of Educational Objectives* (Bloom, 1956) can help here, especially with the last of these points. Within the cognitive domain, Bloom provides a hierarchical list of learning objectives: knowledge, comprehension, application, analysis, synthesis, evaluation. Matching the learning achieved against this list can help you to ensure that an appropriate *range* of learning objectives are being addressed within a lesson, or across a group of lessons so that all students have opportunities to address all kinds of objectives. The same matching process can also be a stimulus to creative thinking about differentiation, for the later objectives in Bloom's list are particularly appropriate for the more able learners.

Bloom is certainly useful, but you will also want information on other aspects of students' learning – did your approach help them to develop skills useful in other learning (for example processes of literacy and numeracy; library, ICT and research skills), what effect did it have on their attitudes to the topic, what effect did it have on them as learners (for example did it enhance or threaten their confidence and self-esteem)? You may also want to ask about the impact on people other than the students – what was the impact of this teaching on you as a teacher (were you totally exhausted at the end of the lesson and therefore limited in what you could give to other classes that day)?; what was the impact on support staff such as technicians; was the lesson expensive to resource?

This prescription can seem rather daunting. However, the really difficult bit is recognising the *need* for wide-ranging data if you are to be well-informed about your teaching. Once this step has been taken much of this data can be gathered in routine or relatively informal ways. If you teach in England or Wales, you can get information from standard tests (such as SATs or end of term/end of module tests) which students take anyway. You will have information from any GCSEs that your students have already taken, and from other examinations which they might have chosen to take. You can get a lot of data about students' learning by the way in which normal work is set and marked. For example, asking students to write about something from an unusual perspective (for example in science, to discuss how far the common evidence for the particulate model of matter is also consistent with a model in which matter is made up of sheets – like a miniature lasagne!) can give helpful insights into understandings and misunderstanding. Whatever the task, you can get a great deal of useful data from it if you look at what the students *actually* write (or say, or do) rather than simply assessing whether they write (say, do) the things you were expecting of them. Even more data becomes available if you ask students to write a brief comment about the work as part of their writing – for example to say what still puzzles them, what questions the learning brings to mind, what they did to solve their puzzles and try to answer their questions, what they *felt* about the lesson. (Such reflection on the part of the student can help to raise their awareness of themselves as learners, to develop their thinking about thinking (metacognition), and therefore support their learning. It is not just an exercise of value to the teacher.) You can get insights into the impact of a lesson on other colleagues by asking them.

Working with the data

Once you have these data you can begin to ask questions of them, and to look more widely at your actions in order to come to some judgment on the extent to which what you did was appropriate.

Obvious starting-points are, 'Did I get the outcomes I intended?' and, 'What unintended outcomes were achieved?' Other considerations are the extent to which the actions you chose to take measure up to the assessment of theories, context and values that you undertook earlier (see the Enquiry task). This is particularly important if you did not achieve your desired outcomes or if some significant unwanted outcome was achieved.

You should therefore look back at formal theories. This may involve looking more closely at the specific theory that influenced you to ensure that what you did was consistent with what the theory actually says (rather than with a general impression of what it is about). However, the main question now is not, 'What was the theoretical basis of the actions I took?' but rather, 'How do the actions I took stand up to the range of *possible* insights from theory?' Maybe you chose one theoretical basis for your actions because it matched your own personal theories most closely, but can now see that another approach might offer an interesting stimulus to a creative change in your working methods. Maybe you can see that a different set of theoretical ideas is better matched to the contextual opportunities or constraints within which you are working, or may be more consistent with your values. Adopting this alternative is then likely to be more 'comfortable' for you, and (probably) more effective for your students.

It is also well worth looking at the contextual issues identified in the Enquiry task. Again, the question is not, 'What contextual issues affected my choice of action?' but rather, 'Were my actions appropriate given the range of contextual issues that I have now identified?' In a similar way you might reconsider the values basis of your actions, then bring the same lines of reasoning to bear on your personal theories related to this aspect of teaching. How do your personal theories measure up to the range of insights about your values system, the context of your work and the relevant formal theories? The stimulus to creative change is then to evaluate what you have done, looking for greater consistency amongst the theories, contextual factors and values that relate to the situation.

This kind of evaluation is difficult to do on your own. It can be useful to enlist the help of friends or to work more formally with a senior colleague (mentor, head of department, professional tutor), or with someone from outside the school or college (LEA adviser, business partner, consultant, university lecturer or friend in a similar professional context).

Re-conceptualisation

Everything suggested so far calls for truly creative thinking, but the most obviously creative steps are still to come. The first of these is reconceptualisation. You have so far identified your actions, the basis for those actions, the effects of those actions, and the extent to which they, and the personal theories that lie behind them, match up to the range of insights from theory, your context and your values. You can now ask, 'Can I think about these things differently?' Your whole set of values, all of the contextual opportunities that you have identified, and the range of insights from formal theories and research can again be the spur to such new thinking. In the process, complex interactions between the three sources of insight may come to light.

A common issue is that different theoretical ideas may point in different directions (for example the notion of general ability may support a system of streaming, whereas the equally well-developed notion of specific abilities may suggest that setting is more appropriate). This can sometimes be resolved by consideration of contextual matters (for example for years 7–9 in school X the timetable makes setting very difficult, but by the time students are in a system of timetable blocks in years 10–11 setting becomes manageable). A different theory gets used in different parts of the school or college (or in different schools or colleges) because the context favours one theory rather than the other.

Apart from changed thinking, you may find that this stage of reconceptualisation leads to a sense that the impact of a given aspect of context is so strong, and yet the outcomes from the practice that this requires are so poor, or the contrast with theory so striking, that something just has to be done about this element of context. For example, your teaching may be highly teacher-directed and in this way well-designed to match the short blocks of time in which you teach, but the contrasts with learning theories such as constructivism, with other aspects of your context (such as students' attitudes) and with your own values (for example that students ought to have a say in their learning) might be so strong that you see the need to challenge the timetable pattern that has been adopted. This can be quite a daunting prospect so it is important to recognise the same analysis that gives you the *spur* to do this also gives you *some useful steps in the argument* you will need to use to convince others of the need for change.

Similarly, reconceptualisation can lead to change in your personal theories and even in your values. The weight of evidence supporting a *formal* theory might convince you that one of your *personal* theories is no longer tenable. One advantage of the steps listed earlier for identifying your personal theories is that the process may help you to see where these theories came from. This can make you more receptive to change when a personal theory is challenged by the kind of analysis we are advocating. (For example, if you know that you tend to do X because X worked for you when you were a student, and you know that your own students are different from you, you might be more able to recognise that there is no guarantee that X is also the most appropriate method for them.) You may even be so struck by the contrast between one of the things you value, and the implications of formal theory, that you may be tempted to reconsider your values. It is, however, worth noting that although changes to your own theories and values are obviously more personal than changes to your working context, the task of making changes can be just as daunting.

Reconceptualisation, then, leads to new personal theories, new elements of context, new values. It is indeed a truly creative step.

The place of formal theories in this reconceptualisation process is interesting. Eraut (1994, p. 29) draws attention to the problem that formal theories can be 'espoused' (i.e. recognised at the level of talk and professional debate), but ignored in practice; or that they can be remembered as something to act upon in a distant (and never quite attained) future; or that they can be dismissed as impractical. Bringing formal theories to bear on the analysis of our actions, in order to stimulate and direct our construction of new thinking, can ensure that they have real meaning for us.

There are always risks in giving examples of a process such as this one of reconceptualisation. The risk is that you may reject some detail of the example and therefore reject the overall process. Despite this risk, I think a 'case study' example may be of help.

Case study

Jenny Smith teaches science subjects to a range of groups across the 14–19 age-range in a large mixed comprehensive school. Having spent some time examining her values (in the way suggested earlier in this chapter) she thinks that she generally gives a high priority to the idea that learners should be as responsible as possible for their own learning. However, one day her head of department asks her if she would mind a student teacher coming in to observe some of her lessons with her 14-year-olds. She agrees to this. After several observation sessions the student teacher asks her to say how she manages to keep such tight control over students' work and why she does this.

In talking this through Jenny becomes aware that her practice and her values do not seem to match. She realises that she has been working with a personal theory that 'responsibility is fine for students post 16, but 14-year-olds are too immature for this responsibility'. However, an evaluation of her teaching reveals that her 14-year-old students are angry about the extent to which they feel ignored in her lessons; she also realises that their written work rarely goes beyond the parameters which she defines – even when these are quite restrictive – so she is not being as effective as she had hoped. Jenny's work on the context in which she teaches reveals that a prevalent attitude amongst colleagues is that 'younger students will always take the easy way out'. She recognises that this contextual issue is actually the reason for her chosen approach, and has sufficient insight to see that her personal theory about 'age for responsibility' is a way of rationalising her unwillingness to act against this general attitude of colleagues in spite of her own values.

However, Jenny comes to understand that, in view of the outcomes that are being achieved (or not achieved!), something needs to change.

She may look to formal theories in the literature which tackle student-centred learning (for example, Fisher, 1997), find out how other teachers have been effective in giving students (including very young learners) responsibility, and decide that she was indeed wrong to limit the application of her values to students post 16. She begins to change her thinking to the view that all students benefit from responsibility. She decides to try something out in her own classroom as an experiment, taking inspiration for the change from teachers' practice as described in the literature. She evaluates her trial and discovers that students generally like the approach and that higher quality work is produced.

However, she recognises that this style of teaching is likely to be difficult to sustain as it is not part of the norm for the students. She then decides to talk to colleagues to influence their attitudes so that this alternative way of working can be more readily accepted within the school. In doing so she makes some limited use of theories of teacher change.

In this process, Jenny has been creative in analysing her actions and the reasons for those actions; she has been creative in changing her thinking and her practice; she has recognised the need to change the context and has been creative about how to do this.

Planning

A final issue is how to make all of this creative analysis and rethinking have a real impact on what you do. One option is simply to rely on the process to filter through into your day-to-day practice so that you become proficient in thinking about your work as you do it and in making changes to your practice, in real time, within your lessons. Certainly Griffiths and Tann (1991) suggest that the ability to engage in reflection in the real time situation of the classroom is one mark of an expert practitioner. However, this is undoubtedly a demanding thing to expect of a teacher because of the complexity of the process and the complexity of the classroom, although there are things that can be done to make it rather more realistic. For example, you can plan specific moments for your reflection into a lesson, perhaps using a little of the time when students are working on an individual or group task. You can become disciplined in using such opportunities to make real time changes in your plans for the rest of the lesson, or for noting down points that you can use later for more measured reflection.

However, I would argue that, even for experts, to rely solely on developing an ability to reflect in real time is unwise. Eraut (1994, p. 53) points out that, unlike many other professionals, teachers have very little time in which to make decisions on their practice. Action in the classroom is what he describes as 'hot action'. The 'pressure for action is immediate and to hesitate is to lose'. Eraut states that it is in 'cooler' action that 'the consideration of new ideas is much more feasible' and opportunities for experimentation are more likely to be taken. This would seem to point to lesson planning, rather than active teaching, as the point at which the reflective process can bring about the most significant changes.

In a sense the evaluation that has been described above, and the creative thinking during planning that this could generate, can be seen as the expert version of the skills which, in simpler form, are so emphasised in initial teacher education. For the student teacher the process of evaluation and planning (informed by the ideas set out above) is necessary because every aspect of teaching is problematic and explicit decisions have to be made about everything that is done. Nothing comes to mind automatically as a result of mental videos which, for the experienced teacher, capture past experience of similar teaching situations. For the student teacher there is time (even if they rarely recognise it) and there is support to help them with reflection even from their position of relative inexperience. For the experienced teacher, planning and evaluation using the ideas above can be so much more powerful, capitalising on a much more sophisticated set of personal theories, more developed powers of evaluation, a more critical awareness of a greater range of formal theories (especially for experienced teachers who are, or have been, engaged in study such as a masters qualification) and a deeper understanding of context. Sophisticated planning does not, of course, have to be as widely employed by the expert teacher as it does by the student teacher: for the expert, some things *can* be done on the basis of experience with relatively little forethought. However, when something emerges as problematic or unsatisfying for an experienced teacher, the reflective approach can be brought to bear on that issue in the ways described above.

However, one problem for the experienced teacher is lack of time. This is a different kind of time problem to that of the need for instantaneous action in the course of a lesson; it is simply the incontrovertible fact that educational institutions have become extremely busy places and there are a limited number of working hours in any day. Planning has to compete for these hours against other pressing demands such as marking.

Another problem is lack of support. The experienced teacher rarely has ready access to an extensive professional library or to colleagues whose main responsibilities are for the development and dissemination of theoretical ideas. One way of tackling this is to set up strong working links between universities and schools (see for example Haggarty and Postlethwaite, 1995; Postlethwaite and Haggarty, 1998). Another is to engage in a programme of professional development leading to a recognised qualification. It is often possible to adopt an action research stance to the development of personal practice as the research element within that programme. This is consistent with Griffiths and Tann's point that, in addition to real time reflectivity, long-term reflectivity within the rigours of fully developed research is another example of expert use of the reflective practice approach.

A good way to begin to act on the creative ideas generated through a reflective approach is, then, through lesson planning. This then leads on to further cycles of action, evaluation, reconceptualisation and (ultimately) more planning.

Being ready for the difficulties

In the previous section, I have drawn attention to some of the reasons why reflection can be difficult and have mentioned some possible ways forward. It is important to realise that there are other, possibly more fundamental reasons, for expecting reflection to be difficult. One arises as a result of the significance of our personal theories. These conjure up images of our classrooms in which things are ordered; we are in control because we have ways of predicting what will happen. There is, as Eraut (1994) points out, a considerable emotional 'charge' in such an image. We should recognise that careful analysis may point to the need to think differently, but it will take a real personal commitment to creativity to be willing to put personal theories to the test and engage in creative change when they fail to measure up, for to do so is to bring a larger measure of uncertainty into our day-to-day practice.

Another issue is that reflection is likely to put individuals more at odds with the culture which provides the context for their work (Osterman and Kottkamp, 1993). This culture may be your personal 'educational culture' (that is, your expectations and background), or it may be the UK educational culture in general, or (as in the case study quoted above) it could be your particular school or college context. This could mean, for example, that while reflective practice enhances learning in your classes, it may also increase your personal sense of unease.

A different point is made by Schön: that reflection begins with a recognition of error which, 'with its resulting uncertainty can become a source of discovery rather than an occasion for self-defence'. As we know from our students' attempts to avoid confronting their problems with a piece of learning, it is hard to see 'error' in this positive way. It is more comfortable to *explain away* the error in ways that protect self-esteem. Even if you can see error as an opportunity for learning, it can still be hard to tolerate the uncertainty involved in thinking widely about the problem, and in trying out possible solutions. It is easier to appeal to (so-called) authoritative guidance which is assumed to be able to solve the problem for you.

Zeichner and Liston (1987) also point out that reflection implies, and is consistent with, 'greater teacher autonomy and increasing democratic participation'. This would seem to be consistent with the view that reflection implies and perhaps requires a 'flatter' authority structure than is often found in schools and colleges. However, as is pointed out elsewhere (Amos and Postlethwaite, 1996):

> *The current educational climate in the UK is not in sympathy with these notions. Teachers are required to 'deliver' a curriculum over which they have relatively little influence and which is constrained by law. They are encouraged to follow a lead 'back to basics' with emphasis on traditional teaching styles. This climate is not one in which the reflective approach can be expected to lead to comfortable outcomes which will keep the teacher in the mainstream of opinion.*

Given these fundamental (rather than procedural) difficulties, it is tempting to argue that we should not persist with a reflective practitioner model. However, some of the characteristics of reflection help us to avoid this conclusion:

> *First it (reflection) is a means to teacher autonomy and democratic involvement. Secondly, as Zeichner and Liston (1987) point out, . . . its aim is for teachers 'to be free from the unwarranted control of unjustified beliefs, unsupportable attitudes and the paucity of abilities which can prevent (them) from taking charge of (their) lives'. Thirdly, Dewey contrasts reflection with routine which is guided by tradition, external authority and circumstance. Finally, Zeichner and Liston argue that 'the kind of changes which we are working for within teacher education and schooling (through the process of reflection) clearly represent only a beginning toward what will ultimately be necessary for the creation of a more sane, just and humane society'.*
> (Amos and Postlethwaite, 1996)

Such a view surely suggests that, whatever the difficulties, there is as yet no justifiable alternative to the search for creativity through reflective practice. Whether formalised through work for a higher degree or not, this approach to the development of teaching, is, perhaps, a way in which teaching can measure up to recent demands that it becomes a research-based profession. The approach makes use of research methods in evaluating action and exploring personal thinking. It also makes use of formal research findings. But more than that, the reflective process described here is itself a research process, creating new understanding through systematic enquiry. The exciting thing is to engage in the process and see just how liberating it proves to be.

Acknowledgment

I am grateful to Sandra Amos of the University of Reading for invaluable discussion of most of these ideas in the past.

References

AMOS, S. and POSTLETHWAITE, K. (1996) 'Reflective teaching in initial teacher education', *Journal of Teacher Development*, **5**, 3, pp. 11–22.

BLOOM, B. S. (1956) *Taxonomy of Educational Objectives*, New York: David McKay Co. Inc.

ERAUT, M. (1994) *Developing Professional Knowledge and Competence*, London: Falmer Press.

FISHER, J. (1997) *Starting from the Child*, Milton Keynes: Open University Press.

FRANSELLA, F. and BANNISTER, D. (1977) *A Manual for Repertory Grid Techniques*, London: Academic Press.

GRIFFITHS, M. and TANN, S. (1991) 'Ripples in the reflection', in LOMAX, P. (ed.) *BERA Dialogues*, **5**, pp. 82–101.

HAGGARTY, L. and POSTLETHWAITE, K. (1995) 'Working as consultants on school-based, teacher-identified problems', *Educational Action Research*, **3**, 2 pp. 169–81.

KELLY, G. (1955) *The Psychology of Personal Constructs*, New York: Norton.

OSTERMAN, K. and KOTTKAMP, R. (1993) *Reflective Practice for Educators – Improving Schooling Through Professional Development*, Newbury Park, California: Corwin Press.

POSTLETHWAITE, K. and HAGGARTY, L. (1998) 'Towards effective and transferable learning in secondary school: the development of an approach based on mastery learning', *British Educational Research Journal*, **24**, 3, pp. 333–53.

SCHÖN, D. A. (1983) *The Reflective Practitioner*, London: Temple Smith.

ZEICHNER, K. and LISTON, D. (1987) 'Teaching student teachers to reflect', *Harvard Educational Review*, **57**, 1, pp. 23–48.

Further reading

Schön, D. (1991) *The Reflective Turn: Case studies in and on educational practice*, New York: Teachers' College Press.

Provides some fascinating insights into the ways in which teachers (and other professionals) respond to problems, and develop both their practice and their understanding. Two of the chapters draw attention to the way in which institutional context affects professionals' actions; one is especially concerned with ways in which teachers reconceptualise their teaching over time. Though these are perhaps the parts of Schön's book that link most closely to the present chapter, the whole work will be of interest.

Elliot, J. (1991) *Action Research for Educational Change*, Milton Keynes: Open University Press.

O'Hanlon, C. (1996) *Professional Development Through Action Research in Educational Settings*, London: Falmer Press.
These explore the idea of action research as an approach to teachers' professional development. They offer a valuable extension of some of the ideas in this chapter, and present arguments that set up a critical analysis of some of those ideas.

| Chapter 4 | # A creative approach to teaching methods
David James |

Introduction

What is the range of teaching methods available? How do you decide which teaching methods to use? Are some methods better than others, or just more fashionable? Some people who are relatively new to teaching become frustrated by the fact that no one seems prepared to give them an instruction manual with definitive answers to these and similar questions. 'Surely', they might say, 'there are optimum conditions for learning, derived from psychological research?' Or again, 'why can't someone just tell me how to do it?' These and similar questions (or feelings) are quite common, and in large part they stem from the real anxiety felt by virtually anyone confronting a new and complex task, yet they are also the product of the nature of professional knowledge, discussed in Chapter 7 of this book. The popular image of the discipline of psychology is unhelpful here, in that it seems to promise 'the answers' (via a definitive knowledge about 'what makes people tick') whilst in reality it shares the limitations of most other fields of knowledge.

In fact, there are lots of tasks we do in life without an instruction manual. Some of them are like teaching, in that they are highly complex and contingent. Parenting is probably the most obvious example, yet despite the continuing demand for books about raising children, few new parents would expect to buy and read an instruction manual and then find themselves to be fully fledged parents, ready for the large number of challenges that are likely to come their way.

If it is not possible to reduce the choice and use of teaching methods to something that could be expressed in 'cookbook' form, what can be done that will nevertheless be of use to you if you are relatively new to teaching? The objectives here are

1 to help you think through some possibilities by looking at analogous situations (some your own and some from the experiences of others), and

2 to help you strengthen your capacity to make reasonable choices and decisions with regard to teaching methods.

Some theories and concepts will be introduced to help in this process, though these are only intended to be examples. There is no sense in which this chapter aims to provide an overview of learning theories or to advocate one particular school of psychological thinking over another. The intention is to generate meaningful reflection and development, to inspire and open up creative thinking rather than to try to be comprehensive or to persuade with regard to a particular set of ideas about teaching and learning. In sum, the purpose here is to promote what Kneller called 'preparation' (Kneller, 1965) and what Brookfield (1987) called 'exploration' and 'developing alternative perspectives' (see Chapter 2 in this volume).

How can we think about teaching methods?

There are small pockets of the education system where it can feel impolite to talk about teaching and teaching methods, although this is changing, partly in response to the various systems now in place for measuring the quality of teaching in schools, colleges and universities. Connected to this, there is still some tendency to see teaching and learning as less 'problematic' the further one goes upwards in an academic hierarchy, even within institutions. This is quite well evidenced and documented in the case of higher education (see for example Becher, 1989; James, 1996) and anecdotal evidence would suggest there are parallels in the further education and secondary curriculum. Hopefully, the trend is no longer as clear-cut as it was in an account of French higher education first published in 1964:

 . . . when we try to make teaching more effective by clarifying its goals and the conditions needed to improve its efficiency, we clash with the pedagogical philosophy of academics, whose disdain for the

> *elementary nature of a reflexive pedagogy reflects the superior level of the education system which they occupy.* (Bourdieu et al., 1994, p. 6)

Having said this, it is probably impossible to teach anything without some thought about teaching methods. Even a teacher who conceives of their work purely in terms of the transmission of subject matter or content, and the achievement of *coverage* in the time available, will need to plan the *pace* at which they cover the syllabus. They may be required by the institution or their colleagues to produce a scheme of work or a programme. They may do this by allocating different amounts of time to different content or by simply dividing the content by the number of sessions available. This is likely to involve the notion of *sequencing* too, because there are usually parts of a module or syllabus that seem to need to come before other parts. Decisions like these are to do with teaching methods in the broadest sense. However, it is usually at a more immediate level that teaching methods enter into preparing for teaching: at the level of what to do with a group of students when we meet them for a period which is usually somewhere between forty-five minutes and two hours.

One way to deal with choice of methods might be to use *variety* and *activity* as one's guiding principles. Most teachers and most students would probably agree that variety and activity are good things. You might decide to divide up the time you have with a group so that the students are not doing the same thing all the time. Students might begin by hearing a short lecture on the main topic, then they may have some written or verbal questions based on the content of the lecture, followed by a discussion in which all members of the group compare their answers and which you as the tutor sum up. But just choosing to 'vary things' or 'keep the students busy' are more like vague intentions than principles. Awkward questions remain, such as 'why?' or 'for what purpose?' Answering these requires that we go a little deeper into basic assumptions about what we are trying to do.

In his book *Learning to Teach in Higher Education*, Ramsden (1992) provides an exploration of some of these assumptions, offering us a distinction between three broad types of teachers' thinking about teaching. The first, called 'teaching as telling or transmission' is quite widespread and is where teaching is conceived as the efficient transmission by subject experts of large amounts of information or the demonstration of sets of procedures. If students do not learn as much as expected, this is generally attributed to the failure of learners to cope, or to their general ability or personality, or perhaps to the inadequacies of a previous educational process.

Occasionally it will be attributed to the volume of material to be covered relative to the opportunities there are to make it all memorable. In this view, subject knowledge is seen as quite distinct from teaching, and teaching itself can be reduced to a set of techniques or competencies. Certain kinds of 'technical fix' are seen as attractive for what they might offer in making the transmission of information more efficient. Learning is rarely discussed and is assumed to be an additive process of memorising content, and therefore relatively passive for the learners.

The transmission theory of teaching has been heavily criticised for its reliance on questionable models of learning and knowledge (see, for example, Swann, 1998). There is also widespread dissatisfaction amongst teachers with the approach, and especially with the passivity it seems to assume – or in practice, induce – in learners. In order to get away from it some teachers have reacted by trying to make their students as *active* or as *busy* as possible. Here, in what Ramsden calls 'theory two',

> *. . . the focus moves away from the teacher towards the student. Teaching is seen as a supervision process involving the articulation of techniques designed to ensure that students learn . . . Student learning is now seen as a perplexing problem. How can ideals (developing independence and critical thinking, teaching in a way that is more exciting than the teaching that oneself experienced, etc.) be translated into reality? Activity in students is regarded as the panacea.*
>
> (Ramsden, 1992, p. 113)

Ramsden warns that this approach is driven as much by the desire for a fail-safe repertoire of techniques as it is by the notion of student-centredness, and that as a result it is seriously limited. We will return to Ramsden's third set of teacher theories shortly. For the moment, we are considering the issues of learner activity and variety in teaching methods. The idea of maintaining variety can be justified with common-sense arguments or with those derived from the psychological study of perception, cognition, attention and information processing. Varying teaching methods would also seem to be justified by theories of learning which attempt to categorise learners along the lines of differences in personality or learning preference. Two examples of the latter would be *Accelerated*

Learning (which distinguishes between visual, auditory and kinesthetic preferences – see for example Rose, 1985; Smith, 1996) and the work on *Learning Styles* which suggests that learners may be differentiated by preferences in the way they deal with information during learning: they are 'reflectors', 'pragmatists' or 'theorists', for example (see Honey and Mumford, 1992).

Concepts drawn from psychological or educational research can and often do inform teachers in their decisions and actions, but teachers are also responding to a range of other agendas, including: the way in which the aims, objectives or learning outcomes are expressed, both formally and informally; the teacher's impressions of the needs, abilities and motivation of the students; the way in which learners will be assessed; and their knowledge of what a group of students has experienced elsewhere in the course, or earlier in the day. Institutional policies (on equal opportunities, for example) might well have an impact, as would the way in which the establishment is managed and whether or not student retention has direct financial, marketing or other implications. Teachers and students will have their own curricula intentions as well, whether or not these coincide with the officially sanctioned ones and whether or not there is an attempt to make them explicit and formalise them in a *learning contract*. Such intentions will reflect the values and previous experiences of the people involved and the extent to which they have developed a taste for being creative with the tasks before them. Finally, we might point to the general ethos and culture of the establishment and its reputation or position in various hierarchies: the list of such variables could go on and is likely to be infinite. As has been implied elsewhere in this book, recognising this sort of complexity makes the listing of 'recipes' impossible.

Reflection

Try to recall the last two times you were in a group as a learner within a formal learning situation such as a classroom.
- Make a note of all the teaching methods you witnessed in these sessions.
- Do you think that the methods used corresponded with the aims or intentions of the session?

With this in mind it becomes clear that even the longest and most sophisticated list of alternative teaching methods will still leave us with questions such as 'what am I hoping the students will learn?' or 'what skills, knowledge and understanding am I intending that learners develop?' In other words, a 'good' choice of teaching methods is only good within a specific context. The choice should be *reasonable*, in the sense of being capable of justification through reasoned argument.

It is doubtful whether there could ever be a definitive list of teaching methods. One person I interviewed recently who worked as a trainer thought that there were just two large categories which subsumed all teaching methods: he called these 'chalk and talk' and 'bean-bags and sandals', by which I think he meant anything informal or which involved direct learner contributions. A more conventional listing would be like the one below:

- Brainstorming
- Broadcast media
- Buzz groups
- Case studies
- Competitions
- Debates
- Demonstrating processes or techniques
- Diaries
- Dictation of notes
- Directed study tasks
- Discussions
- Experiments
- Games
- Individual or group projects
- Interactive CD ROMs
- Internet searches
- Lectures
- Posters
- Presentations by students
- Problem solving in small groups
- Programmed learning
- Pyramid exercises
- Question and answer
- Questions based on reading matter
- Role play
- Seminars
- Shadowing
- Simulation
- Supervision of practical work
- Surveys
- Team teaching
- Telephone enquiries or surveys
- Thirty-second theatre
- Tutorials
- Visits and field trips
- Witness sessions

At this point it is useful to consider the third of Ramsden's types of 'theories' held by teachers. Entitled *teaching as making learning possible*, this transcends the first two in important ways. To begin with, it grows from a different conception of learning and teaching, seeing them as 'two sides of a coin' (Ramsden, 1992, p. 114). Learning is about changes in understanding. Teaching 'involves finding out about students' misunderstandings, intervening to change them, and creating a context of learning which encourages students actively to engage with the subject matter' (ibid.). Subject content and teaching methods are equally problematic in this conception, where they were over-emphasised in 'theory one' and 'theory two' respectively. 'Theory three' grows from a different view of knowledge from the first two, insisting that knowledge is always *constituted* or *constructed* rather than absorbed or memorised. Ramsden connects this crucial idea with the work of Bruner, amongst others. 'Knowing', as Bruner said some time ago, 'is a process, not a product' (Bruner, 1966).

In this view, teaching necessarily has much more of a 'contingent' relationship to the ideas of learning theorists. It becomes untenable to try to persuade teachers to be adherents of one or another of the schools of thought that have done battle for their attentions. Humanistic psychologists (who might insist that a teacher's relationship to learners is the crucial variable) and behaviourist psychologists (who might advise teachers that certain schedules of reinforcement are the key to efficient teaching) can all provide insights that a teacher may find helpful, but they cannot provide all the answers. The important point is that these insights can provide starting-points for teacher thinking, not some kind of scientific blueprint for practice against which teachers' assumptions or practices may be measured. As Ramsden says:

 . . . there are certain favourable conditions for learning which, however, need to be actively reinterpreted to fit specific circumstances, particular students, and the subject matter. The activities of teaching, in other words, are seen as context-related, uncertain, and continuously improvable. Unlike theory 2 [teaching as organising student activity], this view of teaching does not accept that there can ever be one solution, one set of perfect rules, that will ensure learning.

(Ramsden, 1992, p. 116)

As will be clear from this, Ramsden sees this third approach as the most sophisticated. It would be difficult to 'prove' superiority in the classical sense, yet there is good evidence to support the general validity of the model which arranges teachers' conceptions of teaching '. . . on a continuum from information presentation to facilitation of student learning (including changes in students' conceptions)' (Samuelowicz and Bain, 1992, p. 93).

Planning to teach

What would a 'theory three' teacher be doing in practice? Every teaching situation is different and has multiple demands placed upon it. However, let us imagine for a moment that we are planning how we will teach a lesson with a group of GCSE Geography students. For the sake of simplicity, let's also assume that a decision has already been taken as to which topic (and associated objectives) we are dealing with for one hour on one particular Tuesday afternoon.

One approach to this situation is to use the lesson to persuade the students to work through the relevant pages of their textbook (which, in all probability, will have been written with one eye on the syllabus). The summary provided there may well be clearly written, attractively presented and reasonably up-to-date. It may also have attached to it helpful questions or tasks for the students to tackle individually or in groups. If it is not like this, we might consider writing a worksheet – or amending one we have borrowed or written before – that will function in similar ways. Alternatively, we might consider spending half – or all – the lesson giving a lively verbal version of this essential content. All these are common and potentially fruitful ways in which to spend the hour with the students.

However, to be more certain of success we need to find out a little more about the learner's prior knowledge, understanding, skills and motivation in relation to the subject matter. If we know the group well, this will be at least partly intuitive. We might need to ask such questions as: Do the students all have a basic grasp of the concepts? Have they seen other material with which there might be useful parallels? What experiences might some of them have had which will help to build an understanding of the material? How can I use these experiences to good effect? Through answering questions like these, we can begin to make judgments about the needs of our students and then go on to devise material and activities that will have a good chance of helping them to learn. The subsections that follow contain three different approaches to this process.

Learning as experiential and cyclical

Many teachers are interested in the way their students learn from experience, and one theory of learning that many of them find helpful (probably because it seems to have a validity in relation to their teaching experiences) is embodied in the idea of an Experiential Learning Cycle. A number of different cyclical models of learning have been put forward, most of them traceable to the work of Kurt Lewin: however, the most widely known is from the work of Kolb (1984). This version has attracted a great deal of attention, forming the basis for many workshops and courses on teaching methods and providing the underpinning for an accessible guide (Gibbs, 1988), although it has also been criticised for its over-simplification of some learning processes (Jarvis, 1987). In essence, the theory is an attempt to reunite thinking and doing (or theory and practice) which so often become divorced in the organisation of courses and classrooms. The essential links between theory and practice are expressed as four stages, sequenced in a cycle. Learning becomes less efficient where one or more of these stages is missing or where a learner lacks the skills or opportunity to deal with one of them. The four stages are *concrete experience*, *reflective observation*, *abstract conceptualisation* and *active experimentation*.

Enquiry task

Firstly, take a clean piece of paper, and draw a large circle on it. Mark four points on the circle as if you were about to draw a compass. At the top of the circle (north) write the words CONCRETE EXPERIENCE. At the right-hand side (east) write REFLECTIVE OBSERVATION. At the bottom (south) write ABSTRACT CONCEPTUALISATION, and at the left-hand side (west) write ACTIVE EXPERIMENTATION. Next put arrows around the circle in a clockwise direction. Finally, add to each of the four terms some ideas as to what they could mean as activities for your students.

One helpful starting-point for planning a lesson is to 'convert' these stages or steps into activities which will complement and build upon each other while contributing to the overarching objective of the session or series of sessions. At first sight this seems easiest to do where the learning outcomes have a strong 'practical' emphasis. For example, there are several different settings in which UK teachers want their students to learn about the strength of materials (Design and Technology; GNVQ Manufacturing; a number of different courses leading to NVQs). Here, a teacher might apply the cycle by starting with a direct exposure to a critical incident. This could be the witnessing of a dedicated test by machine, or viewing a video clip, or some form of simulation which provides students with a *concrete experience*. Next, the teacher could ask the students to assess this experience in various specific ways, perhaps giving them a series of questions which focus their attention on particular elements of the experience (*reflective observation*). This could be followed up with a sharing and discussion of answers to the questions or perhaps a short lecture, the purpose of which is to locate the experience and reflection *conceptually*: here the idea might be to move students along a continuum which has 'stretch until it snaps' at one end and 'the characteristics of tensile strength' at the other (*abstract conceptualisation*). Finally, the teacher might set up a situation in which students predict – at least on paper if not in some kind of simulation or practical experiment – the outcome of various scenarios. These could be developed by the teacher or by the students themselves (*active experimentation*).

But what of more 'theoretical' objectives? The following case study is adapted from the lesson plan of a teacher of GCE Advanced Level Sociology in the UK, which some people might argue is more of a 'theoretical' subject. The teacher used the four steps of the Experiential Learning Cycle to design a lesson where the topic is the ownership and control of the media and how it may be explained:

Case study: The learning cycle in A Level Sociology

Step 1: Having first asked some general questions to see if any of the students have come across the issue, the teacher used a short video clip of a television programme (where ownership of the media is under scrutiny) to make sure that the students got some direct experience of the issue (*Concrete experience*).

Step 2: The teacher gave students specific questions on the whiteboard or on paper which focused their attention on interpreting the material in accordance with the lesson's intentions, but which encouraged several possible explanations or perspectives. She aimed at: comprehension (for example 'what did the woman being interviewed suggest was the greatest effect of the pattern of ownership?'); evaluation ('why might it matter if the media is owned by relatively few large corporations?'); the affective ('how do you feel about what the man was saying in the video?'). She was careful to give students a clear time frame in which to answer. When they had completed these, she made sure they shared examples of their answers with the whole group. She found she needed to be firm with the few students who tried to undermine a general climate of acceptance (*Reflective observation*).

Step 3: The teacher asked the students to work in pairs or small groups to develop their own explanations or accounts, drawing on Step 2. She encouraged them to use and make comparisons between the summaries in the textbook as well. She made sure she 'visited' all groups to support them with definitions of principal concepts and reminders of connections they could make with other subject matter they have seen, such as functionalist and Marxist perspectives on the media, and sociological research on media influence. Each group produced a short paragraph which summarised their 'theory' (*Abstract conceptualisation*).

Step 4: The teacher redistributed the short paragraphs amongst the groups and asked the students to compare each others' 'theories' with their own and to write constructive comments in response. They shared the results of this in a brief plenary at the end of the session and the teacher collected in all the sheets of paper to help with planning the next session (*Active experimentation*).

This case study shows how one teacher interpreted the stages of the Experiential Learning Cycle for one particular purpose, but clearly lots of variations would be possible within any step of the example given. Regarding the first (concrete experience), she might have decided instead to focus on a case where the ownership and control of the media itself entered the news, as it did in the summer of 1998 with regard to links with Manchester United Football Club. Used with care, this could motivate some students without alienating others, especially if students themselves collected press cuttings ahead of the session. Alternatively, the teacher might have used a comparison of reporting treatments across different newspapers and across media to provide the conditions within which meaningful student reflection and conceptualisation could follow. A good source here would be reporting of events around late February and early March 1998, when a book by Mr Chris Patten, the last governor of Hong Kong, was 'dropped' by publishers HarperCollins on the instructions of Mr Rupert Murdoch, chief executive of News

Corporation (which owns several major newspapers). Clearly, there would be many other possibilities for the other steps of the cycle as well. As a model, it can help open up possibilities for the teacher and the students. The parallels with a creative or critical thinking approach to the problems and difficulties inherent in teaching are readily apparent.

Enquiry task

Choose a colleague with whom you feel comfortable discussing teaching methods and check that they would be willing to help you with a small activity. Begin by discussing with them the steps of the Experiential Learning Cycle, perhaps using the explanation above.

- At the top of a clean sheet of paper, write down an aim, objective or learning outcome which relates directly to your teaching, and ask a colleague to do the same for something that they teach.
- Spend 10 minutes explaining these to each other, and swap the pieces of paper.
- Agree to meet again within a few days. In between, spend some time sketching diagrams based on the experiential learning cycle which could form the basis of a lesson or series of lessons (and ask the colleague to do the same). You might try planning to start the lesson with *experimentation* or *reflection* instead of *concrete experience*.
- Meet again and allow at least 15 minutes each way to discuss the ideas you have generated for each other.

So far in this section we have seen how a particular theoretical idea can be used to facilitate planning where a teacher has adapted its stages for a lesson plan. Of course, there are many insights, theories and schools of thought when it comes to learning. There is not the space to discuss their merits and shortcomings here but it is possible to look briefly at two other examples where published ideas about learning may help the teacher to make informed decisions about their teaching methods. Both are more problematic than the learning cycle model introduced above. The first example draws on psychological thinking about learning of a type that has generated much more interest in primary education than in secondary or further education, whilst the second comes from the North American adult education literature.

The scaffolding metaphor

Lev Vygotsky, a Russian psychologist, was only 38 years of age when tuberculosis caused his death in 1934. In the same year, his book *Thought and Language* was published, though it was soon to be banned in his own country. It appeared in English in 1962 (Vygotsky, 1962), and some of the many insights it contains have since gained a strong foothold in education. One example would be his view of the way in which an action needs to be performed unconsciously and 'owned' in a practical sense before we can subject it to any real conscious control by our intellect. Another is the idea that as we learn higher order concepts, they change the meaning of the lower order concepts we used, so to speak, on the journey. It is this idea, developed via the notion of a Zone of Proximal Development (ZPD), that has captured the imagination of many people in education. The ZPD, in Bruner's description, is

 . . . an account of how the more competent assist the young and the less competent to reach that higher ground . . . from which to reflect more abstractly about the nature of things. To use [Vygotsky's] words, the ZPD is the distance between the actual developmental level as determined by independent problem solving and the level of potential development as determined though problem solving under adult guidance or in collaboration with more capable peers. (Bruner, 1986, p. 73)

In this view, learning (or at least, worthwhile learning) is that which results in development of a capacity to do or know in new ways. The question remains, however, as to how the teacher might make use of this insight. Part of the answer lies in the notion of *scaffolding*, and although Vygotsky did not provide much in the way of detail on this concept, others have given it considerable attention (for example Mercer, 1995; Tharp and Gallimore, 1988). Scaffolding refers to the way that, as teachers, we can structure the space between our understanding and that of the learner, or as Bruner puts it, how we 'loan' our consciousness to learners when we teach (ibid., pp. 75–6). This is perhaps at its most visible when we look through a picture book at bedtime with a child of between 12 months and 2 years and, remembering that on a recent evening the child uttered a reasonably clear 'bird!' in response to a picture of the same, we provide an opportunity – and lots of encouragement – for a voluntary naming of the picture. We are likely to use the same sequence and tone in our statements and questions during this naming game, though the desired response may or may not be forthcoming. Many people do this without much conscious thought, and although there are important differences between homes and families in the nature of language learning, it is as if the 'curriculum' (learning to use the language) and the 'teaching approach' are fused together and somehow come quite naturally to us. In a nutshell, we build little temporary structures which will support the child while they discover that they can actually do something themselves.

Scaffolding may also have an obvious relevance if we teach a *foreign* language. Having got our students to verbalise sentences that illustrate a rule about word order, we might provide them with a series of sentences which are incomplete and which will probably require that they apply the rule to cases arranged on some gradient of difficulty. We might do this via a verbal activity, a gapped handout, a game, a puzzle or some other teaching method. Scaffolding is a good metaphor for the type of support the teacher provides here: like the metal or bamboo poles used in the construction or repair of buildings, it is (a) a temporary structure across a space designed to help bring about some greater purpose; (b) slightly different in every case; (c) flexible and quickly re-arranged, though at the same time rigid enough to be safe; (d) needed in different places at different times, but always wanted somewhere; (e) relatively expensive, so not to be wasted and always in need of careful management – especially in terms of timing.

The relevance of this extension of Vygotsky's thinking is easy to see in the language teaching example mentioned above. However, the idea of scaffolding can seem a little harder to apply in some settings where we work with learners in older age groups. How might other teachers find this metaphor for the learning process of use in their work?

Enquiry task

Pick an area of your teaching that you know well, and write down some examples of the overall aims or learning outcomes associated with it. Then:

■ list some of the *concepts* learners must come to understand during their studies in this area;

■ ask several of your current students to help you annotate the list so as to indicate differences in the level of difficulty of each concept;

■ see if the concepts can be arranged in a hierarchy, or whether any of them 'nest' inside each other or form mutually dependent pairs;

■ sketch out two or more case studies or 'stories' in which several of the crucial concepts are misrepresented: use these during part of a session, perhaps as a 'find the mistakes' group-based competition;

■ finally, talk through the experience with the students and ask them about how their understanding has changed. In particular, note any changes in the way they articulate the concepts when unaided.

I would suggest that there are three related points that are worth making about how the ideas of a ZPD and 'scaffolding' can help us as teachers to think about our work. All three have practical implications. The first is a straightforward reminder that our students are individuals as well as members of a group following a course of study. It follows from this that there is a spectrum of different experiences to draw upon, from the most idiosyncratic to the most widely shared. Secondly, and connected to this, a Vygotskian view of learning reminds us that learners will be in different conceptual 'places' in relation to the material we aim to teach: in order to teach well we may need detailed conversations with students as well as formal testing so that we can locate them on an overall map of the territory covered by our subject matter and desired learning outcomes. Some teachers might find this uncomfortable if they are eager to get on with covering a syllabus, or feel that their students are independent enough to make their own decisions about what they need to know. A few teachers might have been persuaded by certain narrow types of psychological thinking that it is pointless trying to interfere in some sort of natural process in which educational achievement is simply governed by a level of general intelligence within each person. Good information on 'where learners are' requires more than the odd opening question addressed to a whole class ('has anyone heard of x?'): real investment is needed for the teacher to arrive at a useable mental map of the group *as learners in relation to the particular learning outcomes.*

Thirdly, having arrived at some collective picture of the ZPDs of group members, the teacher will need to make informed judgments about how much of the necessary scaffolding can be 'averaged out' across the group, and how much will need to be tailored to individuals or smaller groups within the larger one. This might lead them to produce differentiated materials, or ensure that an appropriate range of choices is given in individual or group tasks. With adequate monitoring of student learning, the teacher can maintain a responsiveness not entirely unlike that of the parent with the picture book at bedtime, providing conceptual 'spaces' which are just in front of most of the students' current understanding. The whole point is of course to take the scaffolding away as soon as it is safe to do so.

Andragogy or pedagogy?

Some teachers find it helpful to think about teaching methods in terms of the age and cognitive maturity of their learners. Although this is never easy, it is a realistic proposition in relation to young children, whose capacities can sometimes be seen to develop in a

Reflection

Think of two children and two adults you know and imagine them in formal learning situations.

- Spend five minutes listing as many potential similarities and differences as you can between them as learners.
- Do you think it is possible to generalise about such similarities and differences?

sequence of stages. There is a very large body of literature devoted to stages of cognitive development, their limitations as explanatory devices, and the application of these ideas to children in school. However, there has been a tendency for developmental accounts to 'stop' at adolescence, where it is assumed that children have begun to think and learn like adults. Of course, the 14–19 period covers an enormous diversity of people and situations and is a period of massive shifts in social relationships, social and legal status, psychological and physical development. There is nothing like agreement about the significance or otherwise of the social and biological dimensions of adolescence, but many teachers who work with the 14–19 age-range decide that they would wish wherever possible to treat their students as young adults rather than as children. This begs the question of whether teaching and learning are inherently different in each case.

Some teachers would operate with the general principle that, other things being equal, a teacher can plan to use methods that require greater levels of learner autonomy with older students. Yet at all levels in the education system one can hear the claim that students have become (or are becoming) increasingly independent or 'responsible for their own learning'. In a final example of published ideas about teaching and learning in this chapter, I wish to give brief attention to the idea that the child/adult distinction has implications for how we teach.

We saw how the idea of scaffolding and the ZPD has received much more attention in respect of very young children than with young people in general. From a different direction, the notion of *andragogy* has gained ground in the field of adult education, especially in North America. For Malcolm Knowles, the originator of the concept, andragogy stands for the art and science of helping adults to learn. Much of his life's work has been devoted to the promotion of this approach against what he sees as the predominance of *pedagogy*, by which he means an art and science of teaching children: '. . . adults have by and large been taught as if they were children until fairly recently' (Knowles, 1990, p. 54).

One difficulty here is that *pedagogy* – the word itself has roots in the study of children's learning – now commonly refers to any study of teaching and learning. However, Knowles uses the term in a specific way. For him, a 'pedagogical' approach is one where the teacher makes all the decisions about what, how, when and if something is learned. It assumes that what younger learners need is to attain scholastic credentials rather than being particularly concerned with the relevance to life of what is being learnt, and that in a pedagogic approach it is appropriate to maintain or even create dependency amongst young learners. The prior experiences of learners count for little, they have a 'subject-orientation' to the content of learning and they are motivated by rewards that are external, rather than intrinsic, to the learning.

Andragogy is based on a different set of assumptions. In essence, these are that adults will weigh up the benefits of learning something before deciding to learn it; that adults will generally be self-directing, even if this is not always apparent in the way they react in classrooms (after a lifetime of exposure to pedagogy); that learners' experience is crucial and a prime resource in learning because it forms so much of the person; that adults are task-, life- or problem-centred rather than subject-oriented; finally, that adults are intrinsically motivated.

Knowles moved away from his early position in which the two models were in simple opposition, with one appropriate for children and the other appropriate for adults. Later work presents andragogy as a set of assumptions and argues that pedagogy is an *ideology* in the sense that it represents a set of dominant, imposed ideas that often command loyalty whether or not people would choose to believe in them. He also suggests that andragogical assumptions can incorporate pedagogical practices, acknowledging that in some circumstances learners will (at least for a time) need to be highly dependent on teachers, whether they are children or adults. This idea is in keeping with Ramsden's 'theory three' (see above), but there remains a real tension in Knowles's approach, because he also insists that andragogy is a response to fundamental differences between the needs and natures of adults and children. The theory has been very influential in a number of spheres, and is probably one of the most important justifications behind the *learning contracts* that have become increasingly common in many areas of education in recent years. It is a good example of humanist thinking about educational processes.

The main thrust of andragogy is to raise the *learning process* to key position, and to claim to give back to the learner control in the area of subject content. However, there are a number of other problems with it. Tennant (1988) looks at the application of the approach in the commercial 'human resources' arena, arguing that it can mean the replacement of a tyranny of content with one of process. The danger here is that ultimately, Knowles is providing a means whereby commercial organisations can dominate people as learners as well as employees. Of more concern must be that the basic assumptions of andragogy are open to a range of interpretations and are of questionable validity, not least because they rest on a very limited evidence-base (ibid.). For example, the 'self-direction' said to be characteristic of adult learners is a generalisation from research into the learning habits of middle-class Americans (Brookfield, 1985).

For the teacher of students in the 14–19 age-range, the debate about the validity or otherwise of andragogy is important. It can help us to re-examine our own taken-for-granted assumptions about how we classify our students. It might help us to make up our minds about our own interpretation of students' needs and the reasons we choose – and indeed hear – for the adoption of certain teaching methods and approaches. Our reaction to learning contracts will be different if we understand something of the assumptions underpinning them.

Conclusion

I began this chapter with the claim that as with other aspects of their role, it is not possible to give teachers an instruction manual that will give them all the ingredients and recipes they need to make good choices of teaching method. I had a brief look at the implications of ideas like coverage, activity and variety and saw how these could be put alongside Ramsden's summary. Finally, I considered how just three of the many published ideas on learning (the Experiential Learning Cycle, 'scaffolding' and 'andragogy') could function as starting-points for productive thinking about teaching methods.

At the time of writing there is renewed interest in and debate about the idea that the best teachers should be given extra financial rewards. Quite apart from the effects such a move may have on overall morale and the willingness of all staff to co-operate effectively, it is interesting to listen to the sorts of distinctions that come to be drawn between different kinds of teachers. As is discussed in Chapter 7, the emphasis in recent years on the use of narrowly defined competencies and standards in the assessment of new teachers has celebrated sufficiency of capability rather than excellence. Yet the dividing line between teachers in general and 'superteachers' is increasingly said to be to do with the least definable aspects of their work. These would include the imagination and creativity with which they find solutions to quite common problems in teaching; the quality of the relationships they form with their students; or whether or not they communicate a genuine enthusiasm for the subject matter.

There are many exciting sources of ideas and inspiration for teachers to consider, both within and beyond psychological thinking. Some of these can be found in the items of further reading listed at the end of this chapter, whereas others might be gained through the various subject-based organisations. Yet it is *how* these ideas are used that really matters. The creative teacher is unlikely to be simply 'won over' by any particular school of thought about learning.

There may always be a few colleagues who will complain that giving serious thought to teaching methods is a waste of time and effort, or amounts to 're-inventing the wheel'. Sadly, this complaint belies a basic misunderstanding of the nature of effort, inventions and (most of all) wheels: every wheel has a different function and solves a slightly different problem. Its strength as an idea lies in the fact that it is capable of endless re-invention.

References

BECHER, T. (1989) *Academic Tribes and Territories*, Milton Keynes: SRHE/Open University Press.

BOURDIEU, P., PASSERON, J. C. and DE SAINT MARTIN, M. (1994) *Academic Discourse*, (Trans. R. Teese) Oxford: Polity Press.

BROOKFIELD, S. (1985) 'Self-directed learning: a conceptual and methodological exploration', *Studies in the Education of Adults*, **17**, 1, pp. 19–32.

BROOKFIELD, S. (1987) *Developing Critical Thinkers*, Milton Keynes: Open University Press.

BRUNER, J. S. (1966) *Towards a Theory of Instruction*, Cambridge, Mass.: Harvard University Press.

BRUNER, J. (1986) *Actual Minds, Possible Worlds*, Cambridge, Mass.: Harvard University Press.

GIBBS, G. (1988) *Learning by Doing – A Guide to Teaching and Learning Methods,* London: Further Education Unit.

HONEY, P. and MUMFORD, A. (1992) *The Manual of Learning Styles* (3rd edition), Maidstone: P. Honey.

JAMES, D. (1996) *Mature Studentship in Higher Education*, PhD Thesis, University of the West of England, Bristol.

JARVIS, P. (1987) *Adult Learning in the Social Context*, London: Croom Helm.

KNELLER, G. F. (1965) *The Art and Science of Creativity*, New York: Holt, Rinehart and Winston.

KNOWLES, M. S. (1990) *The Adult Learner: A Neglected Species*, 4th edition, Houston: Gulf Publishing.

KOLB, D. A. (1984) *Experiential Learning: Experience as the source of learning and development*, New Jersey: Prentice-Hall.

MERCER, N. (1995) *The Guided Construction of Knowledge*, Clevedon: Multilingual Matters.

RAMSDEN, P. (1992) *Learning to Teach in Higher Education*, London: Routledge.

ROSE, C. (1985) *Accelerated Learning*, Aylesbury: Accelerated Learning Systems Ltd.

SAMUELOWICZ, K. and BAIN, J. D. (1992) 'Conceptions of teaching held by academic teachers', *Higher Education*, **24**, pp. 93–111.

SMITH, A. (1996) *Accelerated Learning in the Classroom*, Stafford: Network Educational Press Ltd.

SWANN, J. (1998) 'What doesn't happen in teaching and learning?' *Oxford Review of Education*, **24**, 2, pp. 211–23.

TENNANT, M. (1988) *Psychology and Adult Learning*, London: Routledge.

THARP, R. and GALLIMORE, R. (1988) *Rousing Minds to Life: Teaching, Learning and Schooling in Social Context*, New York: Cambridge University Press.

VYGOTSKY, L. (1962) *Thought and Language*, Cambridge, Mass.: MIT Press.

Further reading

Huddleston, P. and Unwin, L. (1997) *Teaching and Learning in Further Education*, London: Routledge.
A really useful book for those working in FE colleges, whether they are new or established. Contains chapters on approaches to learning and on teaching

strategies, and makes very good use of Further Education Funding Council Inspection Reports.

Pollard, A. and Triggs, P. (1997) *Reflective Teaching in Secondary Education*, London: Cassell.
A good, comprehensive handbook drawing on a wide range of educational research, with chapters devoted to the nature of learning, planning and preparing lessons, classroom management and communication.

Tennant, M. (1988) *Psychology and Adult Learning*, London: Routledge.
An excellent source book on the influence of various psychological ideas on adult learning. There is a good balance of explanation and critique and a wide coverage that includes humanistic, psychoanalytic, behaviourist and cognitive perspectives.

Chapter 5

Teaching and learning in groups
Marelin Orr-Ewing

Introduction

Visiting secondary schools, FE colleges and HE institutions across the UK today it would be difficult to find students who were not familiar with the practice of 'working in groups'. They are just as likely to work in a group on a case study and presentation in business education as they are to have a small group discussion about a poem in English. Group work can take them out of the school or college environment undertaking projects or surveys, or it can be classroom based. There are many teachers who consider small group work to be a crucial teaching and learning strategy, having developed the appropriate classroom management skills to be able to relinquish the 'control' that whole class teaching provides.

If you compare the way students work in a traditional, teacher-led, whole class situation with the way they work in small group activities there are two features which stand out. One is the nature of the students' talk, and the other is the way in which they have to co-operate, collaborate and take responsibility for their own learning. In this chapter I intend to revisit the arguments for introducing group work activities into the classroom, focusing first on the development of oracy and then on the reasons for including more opportunities for collaborative and co-operative learning. The chapter includes suggestions for helping students work effectively in groups and some practical suggestions for teachers who want to set up group work. It concludes with three case studies which illustrate successful ways of using group work across the curriculum.

Reflection

List the ways in which you have used small group work in your classroom over the last few weeks.

- Why did you set up small group work?
- Was it successful and, if so, why?
- Have you any concerns about the way you, or the students, worked?

Reflection

This comment was made by an experienced and talented secondary school teacher of English speaking in 1989. What do you think might have prompted her to say this?

Promoting student talk and developing oracy

 I used to think I'd run a good lesson when the children had been really quiet and I'd managed to do a lot of talking – now I think it's a good lesson when I've said very little and the children have talked a lot!

The immediate reason for change in this teacher's way of working had been the introduction in 1988 of the GCSE examination for English. This new examination included an oral component where different types of oral activity were assessed, including group discussion. This was a significant change from the GCE Ordinary level examination, where there had been no assessment of oracy, and the CSE examination where, although there was an oral assessment, it tended to be of an individual giving a presentation and then answering questions about the content. In order to understand the impetus for this change and many others like it, we need to go back to the 1960s and into the primary classroom.

Piaget's (1970) explanations for the development of children's thinking had had a profound influence on teachers, with his emphasis on the idea of children's 'readiness' to learn at different stages and the importance of activity to stimulate learning. Although Piaget acknowledged the importance of social interaction and communication in learning, it was the work of Vygotsky (1962) and Bruner (1964) that made the direct link between a child's developing language skills and learning. The way that a child learns about language is by using it, and it is the acquisition of the ability to communicate clearly which creates cognitive and linguistic progress (see Wood, 1988). Primary colleagues, particularly those who trained during the late 1960s and early 1970s, have been attempting to broaden the range of talk in their classrooms for many years and encouraging parents to carry on the 'talk' activities outside school hours.

Teachers in UK secondary schools and in further and higher education were alerted to the importance of developing student talk in the classroom through two important publications in the mid-1970s. The first of these was the 1975 DES report *A Language for Life* (The Bullock Report) where the role of talk is defined thus:

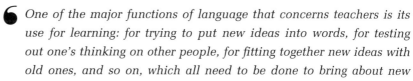

> *To bring knowledge into being is a formulating process, and language is its ordinary means, whether in speaking or writing or the inner monologue of thought.*   (DES, 1975, p. 50)

The authors make the point that if students are taught something by a teacher in the sense of 'being told', there is no guarantee that it will be 'learned'. For learning to take place after 'being told', students need to handle that new information in certain ways, making links with other knowledge and experiences. Just as in everyday life, it is through talking with others, articulating concerns and connections, that they will be able to make sense of new information.

The second publication to have had a major influence was *Language across the Curriculum* from the National Association for the Teaching of English (NATE) in 1976. The function of exploratory language in the classroom was highlighted in this document:

> *One of the major functions of language that concerns teachers is its use for learning: for trying to put new ideas into words, for testing out one's thinking on other people, for fitting together new ideas with old ones, and so on, which all need to be done to bring about new understanding.*   (NATE, 1976, p. 7)

This focus on active use of language by students and the need for them to make sense of what they are studying *for themselves* had implications in all subject areas.

Mercer (1994), writing for an audience of intending secondary school teachers, refers to Vygotsky's work and asks his readers to consider the role of 'talk' in the secondary classroom. Education at the classroom level, he suggests, ought to be about communication and learning which involves participation by both teachers and students. The form of communication which has tended to characterise the secondary classroom, however, is that of the teacher doing most of the talking, either transmitting information connected to the subject or giving instructions related to classroom behaviour. Teachers who set up careful 'question and answer' sessions within their lessons, a skill which was highly valued when I did my PGCE training in 1972, are able to elicit short, basic, 'right answers' from the students but, according to Wood (1988), this type of questioning can actually inhibit students' intellectual development. He refers to research which indicated that,

> ❝ *The more questions the teacher asked, the less children had to say. The pupils were also less likely to elaborate on the topic of talk, ask questions or to talk to each other when teacher questions were frequent.* (ibid., p.141)

The challenge facing teachers is to recognise the importance of learners talking and to set up 'language opportunities' where the exploration and meaning making can happen. Research by Brown, Anderson, Shilcock and Yule (1984) demonstrates that the language skills of academically 'weak' students can be significantly improved through communication exercises and co-operative tasks. The National Oracy Project (1987–1993) was a centrally funded initiative to help teachers become aware of the importance of oracy and to provide staff development training and materials to this end. The National Curriculum Council and the National Oracy Project jointly produced booklets for teachers called 'Teaching Talking and Learning' at each of the four key stages of compulsory education and these were entirely cross-curricular. The booklets are very practical and draw on comments from students and teachers:

> ❝ *If you talk about something a lot it sort of gets stuck in your brain so you can always remember it. (12-year-old)* (NCC, 1991, p. 16)

> ❝ *I found that students talked more spontaneously in small groups than in 'public' whole-class discussion . . . In one case the most reticent girl in the class (or so I thought!) led a group, offering excellent suggestions and drawing out responses from others. (Teacher)* (ibid., p. 40)

As this teacher's comment suggests, once you have begun to organise group work so that 'talking and learning' can happen, the outcomes may be quite surprising.

Learning to collaborate and co-operate

In addition to the views of educationalists and particular kinds of psychological thinking about learning, changes in the world of work have had some effects on how group work is seen in secondary, further and higher education. In the UK, the Technical and Vocational Education Initiative (TVEI) was introduced by the Conservatives in 1982, as a government funded initiative to promote curriculum development across the 14–19 age-range. It was prompted

by concerns, expressed initially by James Callaghan, the Labour
Prime Minister, that schools were not equipping students with the
'attitudes and abilities' to function effectively in the world of work.
School-leavers needed to enter the workplace with well-developed
skills which included the ability to approach problem solving tasks
confidently, communicate clearly and work well as part of a team. It
is interesting that similar concerns are expressed in *Excellence in
Schools* (DfEE, 1997). In this White Paper there is a commitment to
promoting work-related learning because of the disaffection of 'too
many' young people with the traditional curriculum and the school
system and the resulting low levels of achievement. Although there
is no detail about preferred teaching and learning styles in this
document, it does state that there will be encouragement of
'innovative arrangements for work-related learning'.

One of the main purposes of the TVEI was to encourage teachers to
broaden their repertoire of teaching styles. It also sought to encourage
students to take greater responsibility for their learning, to learn
how to communicate and co-operate within the group and to share
findings with a wider audience. Traditional teaching methods had
been criticised for creating 'passive' learners who could, at best,
retain and regurgitate facts and figures but who were not very good
at independent, or team, learning. A characteristic of many of the
training materials which were produced was that they were aimed at
both the teachers (who often felt less than confident about this way
of working) and the students, who needed to see the value of it.
The research and development into group work during the TVEI
indicated that working in small groups has the potential to develop
students' learning across a far wider spectrum than more traditional
methods, and the links between co-operation and collaboration and
developing oracy, noted in the previous section, are quite clear. In a
resource designed to help both teachers and students develop small
group work skills, Jenkin (1986) begins by stating what learning in
small groups has to offer:

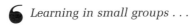 *Learning in small groups . . .*

Heightens
■ *students' motivation*
■ *students' sense of purpose*
■ *students' involvement*

Improves
- *understanding and grasp of a wide range of materials*
- *communication skills and oral confidence*
- *skills of assessing material critically*

Helps
- *students relate learning to their own experiences*
- *shift the teacher's role from that of instructor*

Encourages
- *co-operative learning and mutual respect*
- *exploration and modification of a range of ideas*
- *independence and autonomy of learning*

Maximises
- *students' opportunities to learn through talking and listening.*

(ibid., p. 10)

Setting up collaborative and co-operative learning in teams is new territory for many teachers. In the workplace, in particular in the area of management training, the idea of teams is an important one and the definition of what constitutes a team is not necessarily unproblematic (see for example Adair 1986 or Hastings, Bixby and Chaudry-Lawton, 1986). What does emerge from an overview of the literature is that workplace teams need:
- shared common aims;
- skills which complement each other;
- functional relationships;
- co-operation;
- size which enables mutual interaction and awareness.

Reflection

Think about the group work activities that you have set up in your classroom recently.
- How did you know that the students would be able to follow your instructions?
- What different techniques do you use to divide a class into groups?
- What group size do you tend to use most often, and why?

The importance of teams in business and industry is such that considerable time and investment goes into team-building activities where, for example, colleagues are taken away from the workplace for a day or more to get to know each other, perhaps to participate in activities quite unconnected to the business but which depend on a high level of co-operation and commitment. The rationale for this kind of investment is that the work produced by an effective team is much better than that produced by an ineffective one. So, in educational settings, teachers were encouraged to think about developing students' teamwork skills and in many cases this required spending far more time on the process than the product.

Learning how to work in groups

It is not enough simply to say to a class, 'get into groups', and expect the work that emerges to be what you want and to the standard that you hope for. This is particularly important if you are introducing a group work project or activity for the first time or, as often happens in further education and sixth form settings, the students have not all met or worked with each other before.

In the first instance it may well be worth devoting some class time to giving the students the opportunity to observe how groups, or teams, work and for them to begin to 'gel'. Excellent resources exist which provide ideas for team-building and helping groups to understand the processes which are significant in teamwork. A lot of the activities suggested in these books can be fun, promoting a lot of laughter and good-natured competition as well as fulfilling an important educational function. Below are three examples of activities which, through careful debrief and discussion afterwards, will help learners understand some of the processes of group work. They have been adapted from Brandes and Ginnis (1986).

Tokens and talking

This activity helps learners gain an awareness of the number, nature and value of their contributions to group discussions and encourages listening. Each student is given between six and 10 tokens (buttons, tiddlywinks, pennies) and told that in the discussion which follows they are to put a token on the table each time that they speak and once all their tokens are used up they must be silent. Set a clear time limit for a simple discussion task. At the end of the activity ask the students what they have learned about speaking and listening in group activities. Over a period of time they could be helped to develop skills and tackle weaknesses.

A group challenge

This activity encourages teams to work together against a deadline and with an element of competition. It also provides an opportunity for observation and discussion of the way the groups worked.

Divide the class into smaller groups and within each group give one person the role of observer. Give her/him instructions separately. Set the groups the task of building the highest tower they can manage using, say, six sheets from a newspaper, 6 paperclips and 30 centimetres of masking tape. Give a clear time limit. Ask the observer to make notes on: how the group tackles the task; what sort of talk happens; whether a leader emerges; any tensions; and so on. You could provide a checklist. At the end of the activity, apart from some time spent admiring the towers and agreeing which is the tallest, you debrief and discuss how the teams worked and how the outcome could have been improved.

Ranking

This activity promotes focused discussion on priorities and helps students see the connections between different items or ideas. It also requires the group to arrive at a collective judgment and this will call upon a range of speaking and listening skills. Divide the class into groups of no more than four. Provide each group with nine statements, images or quotations on a general topic of interest (for example – the ideal school, family life, the local environment, pop stars who are good role-models for young people). Each item should be on a separate piece of paper, since the actual handling of the items helps students to visualise the range of possibilities open to them. Ask the groups to discuss what they have been given and agree the ranking for these items. The ranking could be a simple order of importance or a diamond ranking thus

1

2 2

3 3 3

4 4

5

At the end of the time, each group should explain their choices to the class. Encourage them to explain how they arrived at consensus and what problems they experienced, if any.

Ground rules

It tends to be accepted that for a formal lecture there is careful planning on the part of the lecturer and, in response to the delivery of that lecture, students undertake a number of recognised activities such as listening and note-taking. These are 'rules' for what happens in lectures which tend to be taken for granted. Similar expectations exist regarding other traditional classroom teaching activities. A common problem in small group work is that the participants, staff and students, assume that small group work implies informality, lack of structure, no 'rules', and when this happens things can go wrong. As Griffiths and Partington (1992), Brown and Atkins (1988) and Gibbs (1994) all emphasise, there must be clarity about what is expected of everybody during small group work. Brown and Atkins discuss the need for an 'understanding' or a 'contract' whilst Gibbs refers to 'ground rules'. Whatever it is called, some form of agreement is crucial to the smooth running of small group work.

For students at the start of a programme of study, or students who have not worked together before, it can be worthwhile to allocate time to negotiate ground rules as a group, rather than these being imposed by the tutor. For example, a group may discuss the issues for a fixed period and decide that they want ground rules to cover attendance, punctuality, respect for each others' views, confidentiality, the absence of sexist and racist remarks and so on. Some groups will be quite emphatic that these rules should apply equally to students and staff. If students have been actively involved in the forming of the ground rules, they will feel more of a sense of 'ownership' and be more likely to comply with them. The task of establishing ground rules should become easier after the first time and may be undertaken as a matter of course when the students work on group projects or presentations in the future.

Room layout

For many teachers in schools and colleges, as they move from room to room for their teaching, the arrangement of furniture in rooms is a constant headache. Previous users of the room may have left it in a mess, or in an arrangement which is not suitable for the intended session. Seldom will it be arranged in the best way for small group work. To get round this many experienced teachers simply allow time at the start of the lesson to rearrange furniture, calling on help from the students as necessary.

If one of the purposes of the group activity is for the students to talk, then it is better that the tables and chairs are arranged so that students are sitting near to each other, for example four around a double table is ideal. In fact, just moving chairs and people is the least disruptive method; once tables or desks have to be moved too there is inevitably more noise. With this arrangement they can hear each other, eye contact is easy and if they need to look at something, such as a picture or some writing, they can literally work closely together. Sometimes the group activity may involve writing onto a piece of flipchart paper, or handling a number of pieces of paper or objects, and in this case more work surface will be needed and tables will need to be rearranged.

Once the room is arranged for group work, it may happen that some students are sitting with their backs to the board and the teacher. If this happens, it is important that you remember to ask everybody simply to turn and face you for any instructions or input, and at the end for any plenary discussion.

Group size

There are no hard and fast rules about group size (see Bennett and Dunne, 1994). The decisions that a teacher takes about group size will depend on many factors, including:

The age and/or experience of the group
Younger, and possibly less confident, students may need to begin by working in friendship pairs. In any case students who have not got much experience of working in small groups tend to perform better in groups no larger than four. The rationale for this number is that they can work closely together, hear each other speak and eye contact will be easy. In addition there are six clear possible lines of communication. In a group of this size a shy or reluctant student will feel safer and more able to contribute and peer pressure should make it more difficult for an unmotivated student simply to opt out. Teachers always need to be aware of the problems which can emerge in larger groups where one or two group members can be excluded and the opportunities for individual participation are reduced.

The space available
Decisions about group size may also be affected by the space available, how tables and chairs can be rearranged and so on. Certainly, teachers can sometimes make use of other spaces near

their classroom if this is acceptable to other colleagues. The library, the corridor, the refectory can all be used for activities such as preparatory discussions, as long as the students concerned are aware of the ground rules and they can be trusted not to disturb other classes. In small rooms, with several small groups all engaged in lively debate, it can become very noisy and some important points could be lost. It may be that in such cases fewer, slightly larger, groups would work better. Ultimately it is for the teacher to decide what will work best.

The nature of the group task

For discussion activities, smaller groups tend to be more effective and result in fuller participation from all group members. If, however, the group activity is a project of some sort, where a number of different tasks will need to be completed, then the group size will need to be larger and students may need guidance on how to organise the allocation of roles and responsibilities. If the group task is designed to be accomplished over a period of time, then another factor which can be significant is student attendance. If a teacher suspects that there will be a certain amount of absenteeism, then it is wise to make sure that groups will be large enough to function effectively even if people are absent. The teacher's role may well be to help students adapt and cope with unforeseen difficulties and, ultimately, to make decisions about students who are not completing the work properly.

Organising groups

Allowing students to form groups on the basis of friendships may be appropriate for certain, relatively small-scale, activities and may be the preferred way of working when students are new to group work. However, for bigger projects, the advice to higher education students from Gibbs is just as relevant to school and further education students: 'selecting team members isn't just about getting together with friends' (Gibbs, 1994, p. 3). Gibbs makes the point that teams of friends may not be successful because they could be too 'soft' with each other and assume that their familiarity means no need for tight organisation. In essence, Gibbs recommends that teams should be made up of people with a range of qualities and skills and this is a point which should be kept in mind by any teacher who, for whatever reason, has to organise groups for his/her students.

The notion that there are different, equally important, roles within any group or team is one which ought to be addressed openly. In the literature on management training much is written about roles and the problems which can emerge when, for example, there is conflict over who has which role, people do not live up to the expectations of their role, the work connected with a particular role is too much or too little, or people stick too rigidly to their allocated role and team effectiveness suffers (Adair, 1986; Hastings et al., 1986).

In an educational setting teachers and their students need to be aware of potential difficulties and learn strategies for coping. To this end, students could be encouraged to think about forming teams with an understanding of the different roles the task will require, or the teacher could use his or her knowledge of the whole group to set up teams which include students best suited to each of these roles. It is important that any team task, or project, is of sufficient breadth and challenge to justify the team approach. Once the roles are made clear, it should be easier for students to decide on who has to do what and when. It will also validate the contribution of all group members and helps reduce the likelihood of certain individuals dominating at the expense of quieter, or less assertive, group members.

There will be times when a teacher wants a group activity to be undertaken by random groups, rather than letting the students form their own groups, which could result in comfortable 'cliques' for some and others feeling left out. It is useful for the teacher to have a number of quick systems for forming this sort of group. For example:

- Go round the room numbering 1,2,3, etc. and then get all 1s, 2s and 3s together and so on.
- Ask the students to line up in order of their house numbers, dates of birth or height and then simply take the first four to one group, the second four to the next and so on.
- Issue playing cards or coloured cards before asking students to reassemble as 'diamonds' 'hearts', etc., or 'greens', 'blues' etc.

Group work in practice

Three case studies are given below and for each of these there are particular subject-specific educational intentions which are best met through a small group work approach. In addition, the students in each of the examples are helped to develop cross-curricular, or transferable, skills such as communication, co-operation, investigation and presentation. The examples have been selected to give something of a cross-section of situations, with the intention that teachers of other subjects can see parallels in their own classrooms. The first example is a drama activity providing a 'way in' to a demanding text; the second is a discussion activity resourced with reading materials provided by the teacher; the third is a group project where the end product is a poster display.

Case studies

Drama-based work on a poem

The *Rime of the Ancient Mariner* by Samuel Taylor Coleridge is a long eighteenth-century poem which contains a complex narrative, unfamiliar language, and poetic devices which will be challenging for many students in the 14–19 age-range, whatever their ability level. In the English National Curriculum it is clearly stated that learners should be introduced to 'major works of literature from the English literary heritage in previous centuries' and Coleridge is one of the major poets identified for possible study. This activity, which could be undertaken near the start of a scheme of work on Coleridge, will help develop skills such as being able to 'analyse and discuss alternative interpretations, unfamiliar vocabulary, ambiguity and hidden meanings' and respond to a text 'both imaginatively and intellectually'. A drama-based activity also addresses the Speaking and Listening component of the English National Curriculum, providing the opportunity to 'participate in the performance of . . . unscripted plays'. Above all, this activity helps students to get a sense of the whole text before any necessary detailed work begins. It is also intended to be fun.

The *Rime of the Ancient Mariner* is divided into seven sections. The class is divided into seven groups of approximately equal size and each group is given one section of the poem to work on. They are told that within the allotted time, which is dependent on the group and the time and space available, they must devise a short, three-minute, dramatic presentation of their section. They are given the following guidance and a clear indication of how long they have to complete each step:

- To read their section and note the key characters, events and *short* extracts from the text that could be used in some way. To avoid large chunks of text being recited, it may help to put a limit on the number of lines which can be used.

- To think how they can present a brief drama performance to convey these key elements using the group members, limited props and any other facilities that are available in the classroom or drama room. Remind them about the use of mime, choral speaking, tableaux and other techniques they could use.
- To rehearse their presentation.

When the groups are ready, the teacher should organise the presentations to run in the correct order and thus a performance of *The Rime of the Ancient Mariner* is achieved. This can then be the starting-point for discussion and closer work on the text.

A 'jigsaw' group discussion on nuclear energy

In a science laboratory, group work is often simply a number of students working alongside each other to produce individual work. Students are grouped for experiments and practicals because of limited resources and not because this way of working necessarily best suits the intended learning outcomes, although it is important not to underestimate the benefits of collaboration and discussion in any activity.

The 'jigsaw' discussion activity outlined below has a strong science focus but at the same time helps students to gain a wider understanding of different viewpoints, and of possible bias in those viewpoints and to learn how to articulate their views. For a Key Stage 4 group it would be covering many of the targets under Attainment Target Four – Radioactivity, some aspects of Electricity and Magnetism and some of Energy Resources and Energy Transfer as well as addressing the cross-curricular theme of Environmental Education.

The teacher could make his/her own decisions about how the 'base' groups are formed, however the re-forming of 'jigsaw' groups for the second stage provides a legitimate opportunity for different students to work together.

Stage one

The class is divided into 5 'base' groups of equal size. The teacher provides relevant resources for each group selected from books, magazine articles, leaflets and so on. The groups focus as follows:

Group 1: Scientific processes involved in the generation of nuclear energy

Group 2: Key concepts such as penetrating power of different radiations and half-life

Group 3: Nuclear industry publications covering safety, pollution and so on

Group 4: Materials from Greenpeace and other organisations against nuclear energy

Group 5: Alternative technology proposals such as wind, wave and tidal power

Within the time allocation students:
■ share out the reading material and work individually at first. This could be a homework task;
■ identify anything they don't understand and try to reach an understanding within the group before asking for help from the teacher;
■ discuss the main points from the readings;
■ try to anticipate what criticisms might be made against the point of view covered in this group (especially groups 3,4 and 5);
■ make sure they are ready to present this aspect of nuclear energy in the 'jigsaw' groups.

Stage two

Five new 'jigsaw' groups are formed with at least one representative from each 'base' group. For speed this is probably best organised by the teacher but students used to working in this way could easily do it for themselves. These groups are asked to debate the wisdom of continuing to provide nuclear energy in the UK. (An extension activity for more able groups could be to consider if the answers would be any different for another country.)

The representative(s) from 'base' groups 3,4 and 5 should give a brief account of their case with the representative(s) from 'base' groups 1 and 2 explaining how science supports or challenges that view.

Groups producing displays on 'The Rainforest Ecosystem'

This group project is suitable for students in year 9 covering a scheme of work on Tropical Rain Forests. Working in this way should help students develop their understanding of ecosystems and environmental management, clarify their personal values and begin to understand the values of others. In addition, the level of co-operation required to complete the task is high and the students will need to undertake independent research and utilise ICT and presentation skills for the final product.

For this group activity there is a clear time limit and a specified outcome – the display. If the class is not used to small group work, the teacher will need to spend some time making sure that they understand what is expected of them perhaps using some of the activities suggested earlier in this chapter. The groups can be formed according to ability, friendships or by the teacher in order to get a range of abilities and skills. However, it is important to stress to students that they will need to work together to decide who will be the best person to undertake the different parts of the display and they may need to elect a group co-ordinator.

The activity links closely to a visit to a study centre where the students have all had the opportunity to gather specific information. Groups of 5 or 6 students are expected to work together to produce a piece of display material about the rainforest ecosystem. Students are given the following written instructions to support the introduction by the teacher in class time.

'Each piece of display material should comprise the following elements. These can be hand or computer generated.
- A diagram to show the ecosystem of a rainforest. This may be in a systems format or a pictorial representation.
- Reference to climate in the equatorial areas. This can include maps and graphs.
- Plant life in the ecosystem. There should be sketches of the tree leaves, flowers etc. Diagrams to show the canopies and an explanation of the adaptations to climate.
- Animals in the ecosystem – their role in the ecosystem and their various habitats.
- The rainforest as a resource and species bank. Its value to medicine and science.
- You could include some more creative pieces such as poems about the rainforest.'

Students should use large sheets of sugar paper for their display and so pieces of work need to be written on one side only. In addition to accurate sketches of the flora and fauna students could make some extra large masks or leaves to adorn the posters.

Conclusion

In this chapter I have presented an account of the use of group work in classrooms across the 14–19 age-range. I have made links with research into the development of oracy and the changes in classroom practice which occurred following the TVEI. In addition I have attempted to give some guidance on how to set up effective group work activities and provided some case study material from experienced teachers. For myself, group work is an exciting and stimulating way of working where the teacher can often learn a great deal from the students. In my view there is something very rewarding about observing students learning in groups. I enjoy eavesdropping on discussions where students are moving towards explanations or

Reflection

From your own subject area, consider what educational intentions might best be met by setting up small group activities.

What sort of activities might you introduce?

clarifying ideas for themselves. I also enjoy watching their inter-personal skills develop as they learn to listen to each other and reach consensus or gain a clearer view of where they differ. I also like seeing them co-operate to produce an end-product. My final point can be best made by quoting from a teacher who had experienced group work for herself at a conference where she had been allocated the 'observer' role while her colleagues had to tackle a problem solving exercise. She noticed how much fun everybody had had, how the group fell into a silence at certain points and that jokes were cracked but still they returned to the task in hand and completed the exercise.

 An atmosphere of hilarity pervaded the whole exercise ... I didn't give any of this a second thought until I asked my year 9 students to record themselves discussing a project they had taken part in. Before, I would have listened in on each group, nagged pupils sitting in silence and been suspicious of laughter. However, without realising it, I had learned the value of disagreement, witticisms and silences as ways of consolidating and freeing thought. For the first time I felt confident about leaving pupils alone while they were working.

(NCC/NOP, 1991, p. 40)

Acknowledgments

I should like to thank Bernie Fitzgerald, Keith Postlethwaite and Maggie Smith for the examples of group work suggested in the case studies.

References

ADAIR, J. (1986) *Effective Teambuilding*, London: Pan Books.

BENNETT, N. and DUNNE, E. (1994) 'Managing groupwork', in MOON, B. and SHELTON MAYES, A. (eds) *Teaching and Learning in the Secondary School*, London: Routledge.

BRANDES, D. and GINNIS, P. (1986) *A Guide to Student-centred Learning*, Oxford: Blackwell.

BROWN, G., ANDERSON, A., SHILCOCK, R. and YULE, G. (1984) *Teaching Talk. Strategies for Production and Assessment*, Cambridge: Cambridge University Press.

Brown, G. and Atkins, M. (1988) *Effective Teaching in Higher Education*, London: Methuen.

Bruner, J. S. (1964) 'The course of cognitive growth', *American Psychology*, **19**, pp. 1–15.

DES (1975) *A Language for Life*, London: HMSO.

DfEE (1997) *Excellence in Schools*, London: HMSO.

Gibbs, G. (1994) *Learning in Teams. A Student Guide*, Oxford: OCSD.

Griffiths, S. and Partington, P. (1992) *Enabling Active Learning in Groups*, Sheffield: CVCP.

Hastings, C., Bixby, P. and Chaudry-Lawton, R. (1986) *Superteams. A Blueprint for Organisational Success*, Glasgow: Collins.

Jenkin, F. (1986) *Making Small Groups Work*, Oxford: Pergamon Educational Productions.

Mercer, N. (1994) *Classrooms, Language and Communication*, in Moon, B. and Shelton Mayes, A. (eds) *Teaching and Learning in the Secondary School*, London: Routledge.

NATE (1976) *Language Across the Curriculum*, London: NATE in association with Ward Lock.

NCC/NOP (1991) *Teaching Talking and Learning in Key Stage 3*, York: NCC Enterprises.

Piaget, J. (1970) *Science of Education and the Psychology of the Child*, London: Longman.

Vygotsky, L. (1962) *Thought and Language*, Cambridge, Mass.: MIT Press.

Wood, D. (1988) *How Children Think and Learn*, Oxford: Blackwell.

Further reading

Jaques, D. (1991) *Learning in Groups* (2nd edition), London: Kogan Page. Jaques' book provides teachers with an understanding of group work approaches that includes an exploration of some of the theories which underpin this way of working. He also includes sections on group work techniques which teachers can draw on to extend their teaching repertoire. Although written with a higher education focus, this book contains much that will be of interest to teachers in schools and colleges of further education.

Brandes, D. and Ginnis, P. (1986) *A Guide to Student-centred Learning*, Oxford: Basil Blackwell.

This book is characterised by the authors' enthusiasm and obvious commitment to active learning which includes, of course, group work approaches. The book begins with a chapter to set the context and what follows is hugely practical. There are scenarios from 'real' classrooms and ideas for group work in subjects right across the curriculum including Personal and Social Education.

Chapter 6

Assessing creatively

David James with Gaynor Attwood

Introduction

At first sight, the idea of being creative within assessment might seem a little strange. After all, isn't this the area in which objectivity, rigour and standards are the touchstones, and in which there is little room for teachers to manoeuvre, whatever they may wish they could change? In one sense this is true. For example, the teacher of a modern foreign language at Advanced level may find they can exercise some choice in conjunction with their colleagues about which syllabus to use for their students, but the alternatives will not differ in most respects. Or again, those parts of the 'official' assessing which the teachers do themselves – say of a coursework component – will be governed quite strictly by the examination body, and will include some element of systematic scrutiny of grading by that body (*moderation*) as well. Teachers can and do get involved with major initiatives that seek to influence the shape of published curricula and their assessment (see for example Crombie White, 1997), but this is probably the wrong place to look for most of the day-to-day opportunities for creativity in assessment. As will be argued in this chapter, most of these opportunities are in the area of *formative* assessment and in the management of the relationships between teachers, learners and the curriculum.

In most educational settings, assessment (and the prospect of assessment) is a constant, defining feature of these relationships. The idea that assessment defines what is taught and learnt is sometimes referred to as 'backwash', and this can be conceived as a tendency for teachers to teach to the test in a climate where they know their results will be published in league tables (see, for example, Fairbrother, 1997). However, notions like backwash imply an anomaly in an otherwise normal direction of flow. Many commentators on educational processes would wish to go further and would insist that assessment is the only description of the curriculum that really matters at the end of the day. Although they were talking about students in higher education, Brown and Knight's assertion about the place of assessment at the heart of student experience is well supported by other research and is just as relevant in the upper reaches of secondary schooling and across post-compulsory education:

> *Assessment defines what students regard as important, how they spend their time, and how they come to see themselves as students and then as graduates. It follows, then, that it is not the curriculum which shapes assessment, but assessment which shapes the curriculum . . .* (Brown and Knight, 1994, p. 12)

This chapter begins by listing some major strands within the qualifications and courses in place for the 14–19 age-range and looks briefly at the recent Dearing Review. It then introduces some major concepts in assessment before going on to indicate ways in which assessment may be understood in greater depth. Creativity in assessment is a theme throughout, though two particular examples are presented towards the end of the chapter.

Major strands in assessment in 14-19 education

If you are relatively new to teaching, you are likely to feel somewhat confused by the terminology around the various forms of assessment with which you will come into contact. Your difficulties will be compounded by the fact that a series of recent educational reforms has had a cumulative effect, leaving us with a number of different traditions and sets of practices existing alongside one another. In the UK, assessment for the 14–19 age-range encompasses the end of Key Stage 3 of the National Curriculum; the General Certificate in Secondary Education (GCSE); Advanced Level and Advanced Supplementary General Certificate in Education (GCE A and AS Levels); General National Vocational Qualifications (GNVQ) at three different levels; and National Vocational Qualifications (NVQs) at three of five levels. In addition to these, the teacher is likely to come across new Key Skills qualifications and/or longer established qualifications which accredit achievement in a range of areas including key skills such as the Bronze, Silver, Gold and Platinum awards from the Award Scheme Development and Accreditation Network (ASDAN), or the Duke of Edinburgh's Scheme. There are also many specific qualifications that fall outside these frameworks. Each strand has its own history, its own particular assumptions, its own language. An indication of some of the main ones follows:

General Certificate of Secondary Education (GCSEs)

GCSEs were first awarded in 1988, and the qualification combined aspects of the old General Certificate of Education Ordinary Level (O Levels) and the Certificate of Secondary Education (CSEs). GCSEs are the main qualification for students in Key Stage 4 of the National Curriculum, and between the ages of 14 and 16 they study eight subjects. Most of them take examinations in English, mathematics and science, usually at age 16. There are several different arrangements within science, from separate examinations in biology, physics and chemistry, to a single or double GCSE covering all three of these subjects. Common choices amongst other subjects include design and technology, modern foreign languages, art, geography and history. Grading is on a scale from A to G, with provision for differentiated entry. Recently GCSE 'short course' options were introduced to increase breadth and flexibility for a wider range of students. These are equivalent to half a conventional GCSE, but share the same grading system.

General Certificate of Education Advanced Level (GCE A Levels)

These examinations first appeared in 1951 as an academic filter for university entrance. They are now available in a wide range of subjects and are most commonly taken after a period of two years of study beyond GCSEs. They are the most common (but by no means the only) qualification for undergraduate entry to higher education, where a minimum of two passes is often required. Grading is on a scale from A to E. Advanced Supplementary (AS) qualifications became available in 1987 in an attempt to offer greater breadth, and these are intended to be at the same level as the traditional A Level but to require half the study time. A small proportion of students also gain recognition for study beyond A Level by taking a Special Level paper at the same time as their A Levels.

General National Vocational Qualifications (GNVQs)

GNVQs have been available since 1993. They are designed with the needs of employers in mind, and focus on broad vocational areas such as Business; Leisure and Tourism; Health and Social Care; Manufacturing. They are at three different levels (Foundation, Intermediate and Advanced level), and graded 'pass', 'merit' or 'distinction'. GNVQs incorporate the development and assessment of key skills such as the application of number and information technology. The Advanced level GNVQ is designed to be the equivalent of two GCE A Levels, and can be used as a qualification for employment or for entry to higher education. From 1999 a new 'Part One' GNVQ is available, which can be studied alongside GCSEs at either Foundation or Intermediate level, and which will be equivalent to two GCSEs at grades D to G, or A to C, respectively.

National Vocational Qualifications (NVQs)

NVQs are occupation-specific qualifications. They came into being after a wide-ranging review of vocational qualifications in 1986. Most NVQ qualifications came about through the revision and 'kitemarking' of existing vocational qualifications in a process involving groups of employers using analyses of work-place tasks. People gain the qualifications by having workplace performance measured against a list of competencies derived from occupational standards at a particular level. NVQs are arranged in a framework of five levels, though many more are available at levels 1, 2 and 3 than at levels 4 and 5. There is no grading as such: a candidate passes when they have demonstrated sufficient competence.

Other qualifications

Some schools and colleges offer the *International Baccalaureate* instead of A Levels. This award requires attainment in six subjects across the Arts/Sciences divide, and is valued for the breadth of study it represents as well as its international currency. However, there are many thousands of other qualifications, most of them highly vocationally specific, which fall outside the three main categories

Reflection

- Spend a few moments listing your own qualifications prior to higher education, and see how many of them fall into the main categories outlined above.
- What range of qualifications is offered in the school or college where you work?
- Does it seem to you that academic and vocational qualifications are regarded as being of equal value by your colleagues? If not, why might this be?

above. The Department for Education and Employment currently assesses which of these are eligible for public funding. Many are accredited by the Open College Network.

The Dearing Review

In the UK, the body charged with overall responsibility for the promotion of quality and coherence across all education and training is the Qualifications and Curriculum Authority (QCA), formed in October 1997 from a combination of the School Curriculum and Assessment Authority (SCAA) and the National Council for Vocational Qualifications (NCVQ). This body advises the Secretary of State for Education and Employment. One of the most important of its starting-points is the *Review of Qualifications for 16–19 Year Olds*, sometimes referred to as 'Dearing 16–19' (Dearing, 1996). The *Review* made a long list of proposals and recommendations towards the realisation of a coherent national framework of qualifications. The main elements have been helpfully summarised as follows:

- three distinct pathways – academic, general vocational and work-based vocational;
- National Certificates at each level and a National Diploma at Level 3;
- four levels to provide for the equivalence of academic and vocational qualifications, including a new Entry Level;
- larger A-level subject 'cores' and more consistency of standards between subjects, based on regular five-yearly reviews;
- new proposals for an S-level to provide a challenge for high flyers;
- a new lateral AS-level to be taken at the end of one year of study and to be equivalent to half an A-level;
- reorganising Advanced GNVQs into six-unit and, possibly, three-unit groupings;
- a more explicit emphasis on core skills to be certificated within the overarching National Certificates and the new National Diploma;
- bringing together SCAA and NCVQ into a single body to oversee the newly constructed framework;
- encouraging the merger of the existing academic and vocational examining and validating bodies;
- a rationalisation of subjects and fields between the three qualifications tracks, so that the distinctive characteristics of each is clearer;

■ a re-launch of Youth Training within a new National Traineeship framework, linking it to Modern Apprenticeships and allowing progression between the two (Dearing, 1996).   (Young, 1997, pp. 26–7)

As Young goes on to point out, the terms of reference for Dearing's Review spelt out a government intention 'to strengthen, consolidate and improve the framework of 16–19 qualifications' (Dearing, 1996, p. 42): this meant consolidation of the three-track qualifications system which had been confirmed in 1991 in a White Paper (Department for Education, 1991). Dearing was asked to 'have particular regard to maintaining the rigour of A levels' as well as building on GNVQs and NVQs. This was a great disappointment to many teachers and educationalists who felt that the reform of A Levels was long overdue, or who had argued for more radical solutions to overcoming the disparity of esteem between academic and vocational qualifications in most of the UK.

Important concepts in assessment

As a teacher working within a particular strand or strands, it will be important to you to develop a good working knowledge of the way that assessment operates. If you work within a programme where students are assessed in the NVQ framework, you will soon gain a working knowledge of the meaning of *range* in the *range statements* that set some of the parameters for the assessment of evidence of competence. Similarly, if you teach A Level physics you are likely to become well versed in the sorts of clues that may be taken to indicate that students' written work does or does not meet a basic criterion in the syllabus. Such capacities will become refined through experience, especially if you have plenty of opportunities to reflect upon that experience via discussion with a range of colleagues, including some who are external to the immediate course or institution.

However, this approach is arguably a necessary but not sufficient condition for arriving at a basic *understanding* of assessment. Surely, to understand assessment it is necessary to have at least some conceptual equipment that enables a placing of the everyday and familiar within a wider map of the territory. Just as concepts like photosynthesis and pollination apply to vast numbers of different plants and classes of plants, so there are concepts that take us across assessment systems and categories, enabling us to make more informed judgments about the theory and practice within them. A selection of such concepts is given below.

Firstly, there is an important distinction between *purposes* of assessment and *methods* of assessment. Examples of the purposes of assessment would include the four identified in a report of 1988 known as the TGAT report (Department of Education and Science, 1988) (TGAT stands for the Task Group on Assessment and Testing) which was pivotal in the setting up of the National Curriculum. These were, respectively: a *formative* purpose, where assessment functions to provide teachers and learners with information that will guide learning; a *diagnostic* purpose, where assessment is used to identify weaknesses and suggest remedies; a *summative* purpose, where assessment 'sums up' attainments at a particular point (such as the end of a course, or via public examinations); and an *evaluative* purpose, which is where assessment provides information about the quality of provision at the level of the programme, school or college. If we suggest that *diagnostic* is really a subcategory of *formative* in this list, we arrive at three different purposes. These are quite close to *curriculum*, *communication* and *accountability*, three functions of assessment proposed by Broadfoot (1987). But whichever of these terms we use, it is clear that differences of purpose may be identified and that they are important.

Methods of assessment should not be confused with *purposes*. A traditional (hidden) examination is a method of assessment, but its purposes may be any of those mentioned above, or some combination of them. A coursework assignment may be purely formative, or purely summative in its purpose, or it may combine purposes. In a school we visited recently, one piece of assessed work we saw seemed to combine three purposes: it was used *formatively* within an Intermediate level GNVQ; *summatively* so as to accredit key skills development in another parallel scheme; and it also had an *evaluative* function because the school used the result (with others) to demonstrate to parents the success they were now having in developing key skills. The methods/purposes distinction is also visible in discussions about peer assessment. Peer assessment is a *method* which often generates a lot of debate, but this debate is likely to be particularly fierce if the results of peer assessment figure in final gradings – in other words, where peer assessment is being used with a summative *purpose*.

Enquiry task

Ask two colleagues and two students to think of as many different methods of assessment as they can within two minutes: write down what they say. Then ask them what they think assessment is *for*, and once more note their responses. Compare these with your own thoughts on the two questions.

Having established that methods and purposes are different things, what range of assessment methods might be available for the teacher to use? The list may include: hidden examinations; open book examinations; short tests using multiple-choice questions; written course work; projects; a performance of a task or skill in controlled or simulated conditions; individual or collective student presentations; a student production or an audio or video recording (for example a 'radio programme'); a leaflet produced for a particular audience. Although they are all different, these methods can all be made to function with a high level of formality where required. In any of them the process of assessment can be ordered through deadlines, times, dates, places, sources and resources.

At one level, the teacher must do what the assessment regime requires. His or her choices from a list of assessment methods will be greatly influenced by the requirements of the awarding body as expressed in syllabus documentation. If the awarding body insists on an oral examination worth 15 per cent of the marks, the teacher is likely to set up assessment situations that give students opportunities to practice being examined orally. However, awarding bodies are by definition more concerned about summative assessment than they are about formative assessment, and it is with formative assessment that you can do most of your creative thinking about your learners' experiences.

Formative assessment can be seen as a way of thinking about learning and about teaching methods. Whatever you teach, you may decide that one of the main difficulties students have in your subject is to do with a lack of confidence in the way they use certain basic concepts in written assignments. Having decided this, you may then set up a series of assessed verbal presentations at regular intervals through the course, starting with a very simple task but planned with an ascending level of difficulty each time. These might require students to articulate some definitions and examples and respond to questions from you and their peers. Something like this may already happen in the classroom every day, but making it a form of assessment should add some rigour and make improvements much more visible. It may also do much to secure an involvement from all students in the group. We have seen this kind of approach work well on various academic courses but also on a Food Preparation course leading to NVQ level 2. Had the teachers concerned been solely driven by the published requirements of the syllabus and 'rehearsal' for these, they would never have thought to introduce formative oral assessment of this kind. In a similar vein, students on a course which is assessed by a traditional examination can find marking each other's work to be a really valuable learning experience, especially if that work was produced under 'mock' conditions. If they were also involved in designing the 'mock', at least in terms of the range of questions or tasks (something which many teachers keep to themselves), they are likely to learn a great deal about what they should expect in the real thing. Some of the probable reasons as to why these sorts of innovation seem to work can be found in the section below entitled 'Deeper understandings of assessment'.

There are other concepts that are helpful when we try to stand outside the ways we practice assessment in educational establishments. Here we have room to consider just four of them: norm-referenced assessment; criterion-referenced assessment; validity; and reliability.

Broadly speaking, our assessment tools may be based on particular assumptions about how the capacities we are measuring are distributed amongst students. This is best illustrated with an example. Imagine you are teaching a group of 25 students, and the topic is health and safety at work. At the end of a period of time all students take a test, scored on a scale from 0 to 10. The test is a good discriminator in relation to students' knowledge, and as you expect, a few students score very high scores and a few get quite low scores, but most score somewhere in the middle. This *distribution* of scores suggests a *norm* or average exists in what the test is measuring, and that other scores are ranged around this average. The assessment in this simple example could be said to be *norm-referenced*, at least in terms of the assumptions underpinning the exercise. Many tests used in education (particularly with younger learners) are norm-referenced in a stricter sense: they have been developed through trials with representative groups and adjusted (*standardised*) so that the average score becomes a reliable indicator of the most common level of performance – the norm. All the individual questions or tasks (the test items) eventually included combine to show the common differences between learners with different levels of understanding or skill. The outcomes of such tests are often assumed to approximate to a mathematical construct called the *normal distribution*, and this assumption allows a series of statistical manipulations to be carried out on the scores.

However, many assessment practices are built on different assumptions. The employer-derived occupational standards behind National Vocational Qualifications are a case in point. Here it is of little interest as to whether someone is scoring just below or just above average: what matters is whether or not they can carry out a task to a sufficient level of acceptability, that is whether or not they are *competent*. In the health and safety example, you might decide to test for sufficient recognition of the worker's duties under the Health and Safety at Work Act, since this may matter far more to you and to the employer than whether or not the student has a grasp of the finer points of the legislation. Let's imagine that of the group of 25 students, 21 cross a threshold indicating competence against a description and so pass the assessment. This would be an example of *criterion-referenced* assessment, where people are assessed against some sort of description or standard instead of against each other. It is by no means confined to the assessment of occupation-related competence: there are many examples of the use of assessment criteria in making pass/fail judgments, especially at postgraduate levels in higher education.

This particular conceptual distinction is helpful, although in reality the two sets of assumptions often get a little mixed up. GNVQ assessment is essentially criterion-referenced, but there are the categories of merit and distinction above and beyond a simple pass, allowing for the expression of something of a distribution of attainment. GCSE assessment sets out to be explicitly criterion-referenced, though the agencies involved with producing criteria for the different grades ran into a number of difficulties due to the complexity of the task (see for example Gipps, 1990, pp. 82–7). With GCSE and GCE, awarding bodies can sometimes be heard insisting that they operate with sets of criteria, and to reject the idea that they operate quotas of various grades. Yet the relative proportions of results within each of these grades remains surprisingly constant over time. Even a small increase in As and Bs seems to attract all sorts of unwelcome criticism about standards slipping and examinations becoming easier. This is not to suggest that awarding bodies are doing anything improper, but rather illustrates the difficulty of clearly separating the two sets of assumptions. There is also a view that criterion-referenced assessment is really norm-referenced assessment in disguise, because no one would set a criterion that was not anchored in a working knowledge of what can be achieved by likely candidates under particular circumstances.

Assessment methods can also be questioned in terms of their *validity* and their *reliability*. The first of these refers to the extent to which a method measures what it claims to measure. Sometimes the driving test is criticised for not achieving a close enough simulation of real driving conditions: this view questions its validity as a measure of readiness to hold a full driving licence. In education and training there are often debates about the validity of assessment regimes, especially where courses or programmes are being criticised for failing to meet employers' needs and interests.

Reliability refers to the extent to which an item of assessment gives a true picture of the capability of the individual or group being measured. It is sometimes said that traditional examinations do not hold up well under this heading, because they usually take place on one day, and any candidate can have an 'off day'. One of the best arguments for combining different methods of assessment is that overall, reliability of assessment can be increased: the mark the student achieved on their 'off day' will have but a small effect on their total or final mark.

The concepts of validity and reliability are helpful because they make us ask crucial questions about the way we assess students. It is important to appreciate the possibility that in our day-to-day work, a method of assessment can be very reliable (that is, it can keep on producing similar measurements for a given student), but at the same time it may lack validity (in that it is measuring something outside the aims or learning outcomes which the course or programme represents). It is also possible for a method to lack reliability but, on occasions, represent a student's capabilities with a high degree of accuracy. Of course, the problem here is to know which occasions are the valid ones.

Deeper understandings of assessment

In most discussions, assessment is treated as a technical matter of making the right decisions about when and how to assess, given a particular range of objectives and the need to maximise validity, reliability and, of course, efficiency. It is also increasingly common to look at assessment to see how transparent its requirements are for staff, students, and other stakeholders, and make judgments about the clarity with which assessment criteria are expressed. This technical (or pragmatic) approach is probably the most common type of analysis. But other perspectives bring other considerations to bear on how assessment works.

Perhaps most fundamentally, the way we understand assessment depends on the notion of learning with which we operate. In some circumstances learning is seen as the accumulation of memorised material. The study of memory is a vast area in psychology with its own separate schools of thought, and many teachers have found useful insights in the literature on association, or meaning, or information processing models. Tools of assessment may be judged by their efficiency in providing fair opportunities for memorised material to be brought out into the open, as it were. A test too long after the material was memorised could be seen as disadvantageous, as could a 'bunching' of tests of different sets of material.

Other psychologically informed thinking has conceived learning as observable changes in behaviour. In this view, understanding assessment involves a judgement about the capacity of a system of assessment to measure real changes in behaviour. The widespread reform of vocational qualifications since the late 1980s (overseen by NCVQ and now QCA) has put the measurement of performance in workplace settings at the centre of assessment. Performance is measured against elements of *competence* using *evidence*. Some researchers and commentators have pointed to a strong behaviourist agenda in this and have highlighted various limitations in relation to the complexities of technical and professional education (see for example: Eraut, 1994; Hyland, 1994; James, 1995).

Learning may also be seen as the development of the whole person, for example intellectually; emotionally; communicatively; interpersonally. Humanistic psychology promotes this view of learning and gives us another set of questions to be asked about assessment, such as the extent to which it helps, hinders or prevents some of the wider goals of educational processes. For example, we may decide that the most important goals of a secondary school should be those mentioned in the 1988 Education Reform Act that required schools to provide a balanced and broadly based curriculum that would promote 'the spiritual, moral, cultural, mental and physical development of pupils' and prepare them for adult life. We could then investigate the extent to which the assessment of the subjects studied at Key Stage 4 might actually contribute to these overall aims. We may well draw conclusions similar to those of researchers who studied the relationship between National Curriculum subjects and the non-statutory *cross-curricular themes* in a range of secondary schools. They found that 'the subject culture of secondary school teaching seems to have been reinforced by the National Curriculum despite the apparent encouragement of countervailing tendencies in the concept of cross-curricula elements' (Whitty, Rowe and Aggleton, 1994, p. 40).

From a different perspective, John Heron describes assessment as a political issue to do with the exercise of power. He pointed out that a great deal of the assessing that goes on rests on a fundamental contradiction: put simply, we treat our students as highly rational when it comes to learning the subject matter, often requiring them to develop as independent learners in this area. But at the same time we treat them as if they lacked the capacity to make rational decisions about how they are assessed. This is particularly serious in higher education. Heron links this to 'hierarchical' and 'authoritarian' views of knowledge, in which teachers are assumed to be, effectively, carriers of the culture. For Heron, these views are inappropriate if we have truly *educational* goals:

 Unilateral control and assessment of students by staff mean that the process of education is at odds with the objective of that process. I believe the objective of the process is the emergence of an educated person: that is, a person who is self-determining – who can set his (sic) own learning objectives, devise a rational programme to attain them, set criteria of excellence by which to assess the work he produces, and assess his own work in the light of those criteria . . . But the traditional educational process does not prepare the student to acquire any of these self-determining competencies. In each respect, the staff do it for or to the students. An educational process that is so determined cannot have as its outcome a person who is truly self-determining.
(Heron, 1988, p. 79–80)

Reflection

Think about the last time you sat an examination or had a piece of work formally assessed, then answer the following questions:

- Did you have any choice about the timing and location of the assessment?
- Did you have any choice about the nature of the tasks required?
- Did you have any choice about the criteria used to judge the quality of the work?

Heron advocates the increasing use of peer assessment, self-assessment and *collaborative* forms of assessment as the way in which teachers can contribute to overcoming the contradictions he has spelt out. Many teachers continue to find this (and similar) analyses helpful in clarifying their own values and making decisions about what to do when they have choices in assessment.

Assessment may also be understood from the point of view of the various participants in situations where it happens. How do groups of A Level students view the course work components they are required to complete? Arguably, the *reality* of assessment for individual students and groups of students is just as important as anyone else's version of events, especially as the student will usually have some kind of personal stake in the outcomes of assessment. Some sociological studies have approached assessment from this *interactionist* angle and focused on such matters as the collective interpretation of grades and the different perspectives generally held by staff and students in relation to the purposes of assessment. In one American study (Becker, Geer and Hughes, 1968), it was concluded that the system of assessment was characterised by a 'built in irremediable conflict':

 Students and . . . [staff] view the relation between academic achievement and the individual ability of the student differently. The student, from a common . . . [staff] point of view, does as well in his (sic) academic work as his abilities and motivation allow him to do; if he does poorly, it is because he cannot or will not do better . . . Students do not share this view. They think that the student controls his own academic fate by the amount of effort he puts forth . . . they thus attribute variations in student performance to an unwillingness to give sufficient time and effort to academic work or to a deliberate decision to put one's major effort elsewhere. (ibid., p. 39)

The result was that students constantly engaged in information-seeking because of the importance of grades, whilst tutors felt they could only make ambiguous statements in response. If the tutors had furnished the level of detail students demanded, '. . . the function of examinations and assignments as measures of student ability would be destroyed' (ibid., pp. 86–7).

Assessment may also be understood at higher levels of abstraction. We may identify wider 'functions' of assessment (such as the selection and control of people by the state in ways which may reproduce class or gender divides), or perhaps try to understand the sets of qualifications we live with as the product of political processes in which there have been winners and losers as different interests competed. An example of a 'system' view is the analysis of changes in 'assessment culture' presented by Broadfoot. This analysis draws attention to such things as the tendency in mass education systems for postponement in the age at which major selective choices between pupils are made, or matters like the 'international trend towards the institution of hierarchical, criterion-referenced, curriculum and assessment frameworks as the basis for the organisation of the *compulsory* stages of schooling' (Broadfoot, 1996, pp. 51–2). Other 'macro' analyses have looked at *qualification inflation* (Dore, 1976) or *credential inflation* (Hirsch, 1977). Essentially, these both refer to the idea that as educational opportunities expand, the number of people with a given qualification increases to outstrip the job opportunities that were traditionally associated with the qualification. This not only means that the qualification loses some of its value, but it also creates new pressures in the form of demand for more qualifications at a higher level. This idea remains important: it fits well with Bourdieu's notion of educational qualifications as a form of *cultural capital* which is to some extent convertible to and from other sorts of capital, including wealth (see Brown, 1997; Grenfell and James, 1998, pp. 20–1); and it has continued relevance for an understanding of how '. . . higher socio-economic groups preserve and reproduce their privilege by raising the educational levels demanded for elite occupations' (Brown, Halsey, Lauder and Stuart Wells, 1997, p. 10).

Perspectives like those introduced above are helpful to the teacher who wishes to understand more about what is at stake in day-to-day assessment practices. They may also be of direct help in subjecting individual or institutional practices to scrutiny as part of an attempt to change or refine what may otherwise be taken for granted.

Opportunities for creativity in assessment

Several examples of teacher creativity with assessment have arisen in the course of the discussion in this chapter, and near the beginning of the chapter it was suggested that most of the opportunities of this kind were to be found in the everyday management of the relationship between teachers, students and the curriculum. Creativity is always in a context. There is no doubt that some contexts promote creativity, at least in the sense that teachers are sometimes presented with opportunities to innovate. In this last section, we want to introduce two further examples of creativity in assessment: the first arose when an individual teacher in a secondary school saw an opportunity to solve a problem through a change in existing assessment arrangements. This is presented as a case study. The second example centres on the collective interpretation of a new curriculum requirement in a sixth form college, and came to light during a research project that was looking at the successful development of key skills in a number of different settings (James and Brewer, 1998).

Case study

Fiona is an experienced teacher of Religious Education in a large comprehensive school. On the whole she enjoys her work. The GCSE and GCE A Level results in her subject are amongst the best in the school, and colleagues recognise that this is partly due to her enthusiasm but also stems from her careful management of learning. For example, she is well-known amongst staff and students alike for the importance she places on regular fortnightly tests for all her students. These tests require students to write three paragraph-sized answers to questions based on the lesson content of the previous two weeks.

However, she feels there are two problems that are increasing, year-on-year, and that although they seem like small things, they have begun to jeopardise the achievements of the students in examinations. The first problem is that students' spelling of key terms – such as the names of important events in various religious calendars – seems to be getting worse. The second is that in most of her classes there now seems to be a group of students who are very reluctant to participate in discussion.

Fiona has tried talking these problems through with the students, giving them what she called a 'pep talk' on the importance of spelling and contributing to discussion, but it did not seem to make much difference. Then one day, whilst describing the issue to a friend during a long walk in the country, she became intrigued when the friend asked her whether it would be possible to make both issues 'more important' in lessons. The conversation was interrupted before she could quiz her friend about what she meant, but the germ of an idea had been planted.

Reflection

- Does Fiona's situation have any parallels with what happens during classes you teach?
- To what extent do you make explicit use of formative assessment to guide learning?
- Is there anything you would like to change in the way you use formative assessment?

Within another week Fiona had devised a plan. She would make both the spelling of key terms and participation in discussion become necessary features of successful progression, by making these two things part of the regular fortnightly tests. She reasoned that students had sufficient opportunity to develop their knowledge of the 'content' of the syllabus through essays and existing items of homework. The tests would be changed and would now contain:

- One prepared paragraph written by Fiona herself, in which students had to find and correct up to twelve errors in key terms. She prepared this on a word processor, so it was easy to produce a correct version at the same time which could be handed out to students to file with their notes once the test was marked;
- One question based on content recall, as in the old test;
- One question in which students had to describe a contribution they had made to a discussion during the previous two weeks, with a commentary about how it differed from the views expressed by at least two other students.

Fiona put her plan into action and it made a difference. Her impression was that spelling of key terms got better within a few months, and there was a greater willingness on the part of 'quieter' students to engage in discussion. An unexpected consequence was that some students who had seemed to dominate discussion before, now seemed a little reluctant to contribute in their own words, wanting to get phrases from the textbook or handout and build these into their contribution. Fiona decided this was not enough of a problem to warrant action.

In the case study above, a teacher identified a problem and attempted to solve it, more or less on her own. In other circumstances, teachers find they must arrive at collective solutions to collective problems. One example of this was with what happened at 'Parkside Sixth Form College' situated in a large city in the west of England. An increase in the number of GNVQ courses offered, and the knowledge that comprehensive key skills qualifications were very likely to be introduced within a couple of years, led the college to be one of the first to appoint a key skills co-ordinator whose responsibilities covered all 16–19 courses. GNVQ courses incorporate explicit assessment of key skills, with teachers spending time to identify and record instances where elements of the key skills are covered by students. At Parkside the key skills co-ordinator was instrumental in getting other staff to work together in new ways to maximise opportunities for both key skills *development* and key skills *assessment*.

The key skills co-ordinator oversaw the setting up of a major sporting event, designed and run by students but steered by staff. It involved advertising, correspondence, attracting sponsorship, co-ordinating large numbers of events and entrants, the design and production of certificates and many other similar tasks, all of which could be used as direct evidence of key skills capabilities. Perhaps of most interest here is that a particular interpretation of the key skills requirements – as a formative opportunity rather than as a summative burden – triggered the creativity of staff and students in a collective and celebrated effort (for further detail of this research see James and Brewer, 1998).

Conclusion

Like Brown and Knight (1994) we would argue that to view 'the curriculum' and 'assessment' as separate entities is unhelpful, especially if there is a wish to understand learning and student experience. In this chapter we have presented outlines of the main qualification strands in 14–19 education; some important concepts and distinctions in assessment; different perspectives in the understanding of assessment; examples of creativity in assessment. If there is one overarching message in all this, it must be that you can and should be creative with assessment, but that you will need a good grasp of both the context within which you are operating and the problems you are trying to solve. You may well find it necessary to look beyond your immediate work situation to find these things.

References

Becker, H. S., Geer, B. and Hughes, E. C. (1968) *Making the Grade: The Academic Side of College Life*, New York: J. Wiley and Sons.

Broadfoot, P. (1987) *Introducing Profiling – A Practical Manual*, London: Macmillan Educational.

Broadfoot, P. (1996) *Education, Assessment and Society*, Buckingham: Open University Press.

Brown, P. (1997) 'Cultural capital and social exclusion: some observations on recent trends in education, employment, and the labour market', in Halsey, A. H., Lauder, L., Brown, P. and Stuart-Wells, A. (eds) *Education – Culture, Economy, and Society,* Oxford: Oxford University Press.

BROWN, P., HALSEY, A. H., LAUDER, L. and STUART WELLS, A. (1997) 'The transformation of education and society: an introduction', in HALSEY, A. H., LAUDER, L., BROWN, P. and STUART-WELLS, A. (eds) *Education – Culture, Economy, and Society*, Oxford: Oxford University Press.

BROWN, S. and KNIGHT, P. (1994) *Assessing Learners in Higher Education*, London: Kogan Page.

CROMBIE WHITE, R. (1997) *Curriculum Innovation: A Celebration of Classroom Practice*, Milton Keynes: Open University Press.

DEARING, R. (1996) *Review of Qualifications for 16–19 Year Olds – Summary Report*, Hayes: School Curriculum and Assessment Authority.

DEPARTMENT FOR EDUCATION (1991) *Education and Training for the 21st Century*, London: HMSO.

DEPARTMENT OF EDUCATION AND SCIENCE (1988) *National Curriculum: Task Group on Assessment and Testing – A Report*, London: DES/Welsh Office.

DORE, R. (1976) *The Diploma Disease*, London, Unwin.

ERAUT, M. (1994) *Developing Professional Knowledge and Competence*, London: Falmer Press.

FAIRBROTHER, B. (1997) 'Assessing pupils', in Dillon, J. and Maquire, M. (eds) *Becoming a Teacher – Issues in Secondary Schooling*, Buckingham: Open University Press.

GIPPS, C. (1990) *Assessment – A Teacher's Guide to the Issues*, London: Hodder and Stoughton.

GRENFELL, M. and JAMES, D. (1998) *Bourdieu and Education: Acts of Practical Theory*, London: Falmer Press.

HERON, J. (1988) 'Assessment revisited', in BOUD, D. (ed.) *Developing Student Autonomy in Learning*, London: Kogan Page.

HIRSCH, F. (1977) *The Social Limits to Growth*, London: Routledge.

HYLAND, T. (1994) *Competence, Education and NVQs: Dissenting Perspectives*, London: Cassell.

JAMES, D. (1995) 'Universal teacher education for the FE sector: whatever next?', *Redland Papers*, **3**, pp. 51–9.

JAMES, D. and BREWER, J. (1998) 'Key skills across the pathways? Case studies of successful development and some implications for policy'. Paper presented at *British Educational Research Association Annual Conference*, Queen's University of Belfast.

WHITTY, G., ROWE, G. and AGGLETON, P. (1994) 'Discourse in cross-curricular contexts: limits to empowerment', *International Studies in Sociology of Education*, **4**, 1, pp. 25–42.

YOUNG, M. (1997) 'The Dearing Review of 16–19 Qualifications: a step towards a unified system?', in Hodgson, A. and Spours, K. (eds) *Dearing and Beyond* – 14–19 Qualifications, Frameworks and Systems, London: Kogan Page.

Further reading

Hayward, G. (1995) *Getting to Grips with GNVQs – A Handbook for Teachers*, London: Kogan Page.
This is a highly practical book that appeals to both experienced and inexperienced teachers. It manages to convey the relative complexity of GNVQs whilst maintaining a reassuring and highly accessible style. The issues the teacher confronts in working with GNVQs are dealt with under three 'themes' (entitled *basics, core skills* and *the management of student learning*), and the book never loses sight of the fact that different institutions need to solve the problems thrown up by GNVQs in different ways. Whilst one or two details have changed in the few years since it was written, it is still a very good guide, especially for teachers whose main points of reference lie within other types of qualifications.

Broadfoot, P. (1996) *Education, Assessment and Society – A Sociological Analysis*, Buckingham: Open University Press.
Teachers who wish to look more deeply into the ways that assessment has grown and changed in relation to other, major social forces and events will find this book of great interest, especially if they already have some familiarity with sociological concepts. The book deals with matters like the relationship between assessment and the economy, or its functioning as a device for social control. Comparative case studies of assessment systems, policy and practice in France and England are used to drive part of the analysis.

Hodgson, A. and Spours, K. (eds) (1997) *Dearing and Beyond – 14–19 Qualifications, Frameworks and Systems*, London: Kogan Page.
This book presents a collection of chapters by different authors, many of whom are leading researchers in the field of post-compulsory education. The chapters are at times quite loosely connected, but collectively they provide a detailed analysis of the situation with regard to the qualifications framework, set in a recent historical context. In addition to explaining why it is that Dearing's 1996 *Review of Qualifications for 16–19 Year Olds* did not lead to a hoped-for consensus, the book also sets out arguments in favour of a 'unified' system of qualifications and describes the sort of long-term reform process needed to achieve it.

Chapter 7

The professional teacher
David James, Kate Ashcroft and Marelin Orr-Ewing

Introduction

As in many occupations, the beginning teacher is likely to find they
are surrounded by references to the idea of a profession, of 'being
professional' or 'acting professionally'. At some point, whether in
completing an initial training or in interviews for jobs or promotions,
they are likely to be assessed against criteria that make explicit
reference to the formation of professional relationships with
colleagues and with students. The idea is used on a daily basis as a
measure of our own and of others' actions, but what does it mean?
This chapter begins by considering a range of meanings and
approaches of relevance to teachers of young people across the 14–19
age-range. It then looks at the routes into teaching and at certain of
the changes to these, together with their implications. A section
follows which explores the nature of professional knowledge in
relation to teaching and teacher education. Two final sections look at
the professional career in teaching and at continuing professional
development.

What it means to be a professional

The term 'profession' is often used to make a distinction
between certain occupational groups. Most people would agree that
solicitors and doctors are professionals, and that clerical officers and
secretaries are not. This can have direct consequences in many walks
of life, from renting accommodation to obtaining a loan. Yet the word

as a noun seems to cover a different area from its use as an adjective: if a clerical officer became careless in the way they checked the payment of invoices, it would sound reasonable to describe their behaviour as 'unprofessional'. It seems that 'being professional' applies to many jobs whilst 'being a professional' only applies to some. In most dictionary definitions, a profession is an occupation which is non-manual and which requires a period of training. However, being professional can also mean simply doing something for money instead of for pleasure (for example musicians can be divided into professional, semi-professional and amateur on this dimension). It also includes displaying a skill or standard appropriate to a task ('at this garage we pride ourselves on offering a really professional service to the customer'), and even the amateur can give a 'professional' performance!

Broadly speaking, social science writing about the professions has tended to approach the topic in one of three ways. The first attempts to arrive at a list of attributes or functions which might help us (a) to decide whether or not an occupational group is a profession, and (b) to understand the relatively high rewards attached to many professional roles. The attributes usually include: a set of skills based on a body of theoretical knowledge; a well-defined and extensive period of education with rigorous testing before qualification; a code of conduct or ethics; self-regulation; altruism (for instance, putting the interests of the client or public first); control of entry to the occupation. In this view, the high rewards of (say) lawyers reflect the importance to society of the matters they deal with (though the approach was never intended to provide a clear-cut definition of a profession). It is worth considering how many of the attributes mentioned above apply to teaching. It is also worth testing against one's own experience the idea that people's monetary rewards reflect the importance or value of their contributions to society.

The second broad approach is somewhat different and can be seen as being in opposition to the first. One of the most famous expressions of it comes from one-time office worker and renowned dramatist George Bernard Shaw, in whose 1906 play *The Doctor's Dilemma* a character tells us 'all professions are conspiracies against the laity'. This is a powerful expression of the idea that professions 'fence off' areas of knowledge or practices and serve their own interests under the guise of serving the best interests of the public. Here professionalisation is understood as a particular strategy that different groups of workers have had different degrees of success in adopting. Thus, at the point where the state became heavily involved in medical services with the setting up of the National Health Service, medical doctors had already achieved an effective monopoly of therapeutic practices and could virtually name their price. By contrast, the state itself initiated all the major expansions in education, so teachers have relied on trade unionism to gain what ground they could in the occupational hierarchy. In this approach, all the attributes mentioned above appear in a new light. Such things as controlling entry to the occupation to keep up standards now look like the creation of an artificial shortage; altruism appears as an idea which the members of the group promulgate because it suits their interests to *appear* to have the client's interests at heart. In other words, in this view professionalism is *ideological* whether or not there is a conscious 'conspiracy', and it is no more than a specific case of workers seeking to control the conditions under which they work, something that all groups of workers do all the time.

A third broad approach, linked in many ways to the second, puts concepts like *intensification, de-professionalisation* and *de-skilling* at the centre of the analysis. Like many groups of professionals, teachers seem to have experienced increases in the amount of work expected of them and in the gravity of the consequences for them if they do not increase 'productivity'. This intensification of the work-load, in both volume and diversity, requires new managerial skills. Some writers such as Apple and Jungck (1991) have argued that teachers are, collectively, duped into seeing these new skills as representing an increase in their professionality, and that they 'collude' in the intensification of their work. Others, including Lawn and Ozga (1988), have focused on the 'proletarianisation' of teachers as certain skills and autonomy are removed and as more of the conceptual side of teachers' work is replaced by decisions which are made centrally. Analyses like these have been subject to considerable criticism. In particular, the idea of intensification is difficult to substantiate and begs the question as to what is being compared to what, and when. In addition, it has been argued that there is no necessary contradiction between an increased or more complex work-load and increased professionality (see Campbell and Neill, 1994, pp. 159–68 for a good summary of these arguments).

There can be no doubt that analyses which spring from the three approaches outlined are of considerable interest and importance for teachers wanting to understand their social, historical and economic location. However, their primary concern is with understanding aspects of professions as groups of workers, even when they draw directly on accounts of what professionals do. The concerns of this book are somewhat different, in that we seek to help teachers to explore and develop their own definitions of professionality. Professional action and professional knowledge may of course be studied as elements of broader socio-economic change but they also have a much more immediate resonance, visible in the practices of teachers and the ways they relate to students, colleagues and others. The rest of this chapter explores these meanings under a number of headings.

Changing routes to a professional qualification

There are a variety of routes to becoming a teacher in England and Wales. A number of these have been developed recently, and have come about as a result of changes in the conception of what it is to be a teacher. There are two main senses in which these routes are likely to have significance for you as a developing professional. On the one hand, an understanding of the basis of the models of training may help you to appreciate the strengths and limitations of your own training, and so help you to consider what further development might complement it. Alternatively, you might be interested in developing your professionalism as a qualified teacher through supporting student teachers or other inexperienced colleagues, in which case an overview of recent developments will help you to locate the role you might play.

In the UK, the 14–19 age-range includes a variety of institutional arrangements, each with a distinctive history, and there is no simple summary of the routes into teaching. Depending on the type of institution and the nature of the course, there may or may not be a statutory requirement for the teacher to be qualified. Secondary schools in the state sector will generally employ qualified teachers, but this requirement does not automatically apply to independent schools, further education colleges, or in higher education, though there are many changes afoot, at least in respect of the last two of these. In many cases institutions themselves have requirements and, other things being equal, it is usually the case that a teaching qualification will help someone gain employment and promotion, whatever kind of educational establishment they work in.

For teaching in secondary schools, the most common routes are the three or four year undergraduate training (usually leading to a degree [BEd or BA/BSc Hons] with Qualified Teacher Status [QTS]), and for those with a relevant degree, the one year post graduate certificate (PGCE), again with QTS. These are mostly organised and run from colleges of higher education and universities, and operated in partnership with schools. For teaching in the further education sector, the most usual route is via a further education teaching certificate (Cert. Ed. [FE]), generally operated as a two year in-service training course (though available in some places as a one-year full-time course), run and validated by a university. However, some teachers still begin teaching in the FE sector without any teaching qualification. Often they will study part-time alongside their new job to gain a basic skills-focused qualification known as the Further and Adult Education Teachers' Certificate, and they may go on to do the Cert. Ed. (FE) or a similar higher education qualification afterwards.

During the 1980s and 1990s, the government developed a number of alternative routes into teaching for those wishing to teach in schools. These include School-Centred Initial Teacher Training initiatives, which may or may not involve higher education and the (now largely discontinued) Articled Teacher Scheme (a part-time school-based route operated in co-operation with higher education) and Graduate and Registered Teacher schemes (on-the-job training schemes for unqualified teachers in employment).

The development of models of school-based training was accompanied by increasing regulation of the more established, higher education routes into school teaching. This regulation included requirements for more time in school and a greater involvement of teachers in training processes, more emphasis on subject knowledge and subject specialism and increasingly specific and demanding curriculum requirements, especially in relation to the core curriculum and information and communication technology. One result of this has been to squeeze the time for reflection and discussion of general and wider professional issues, particularly those that are concerned with ethics and values.

The model of teacher training thus has moved towards an apprenticeship model, which has much in common with that described by Hargreaves (1996) as 'pre-professional' and current during the first half of the twentieth century. Pre-professional training was largely based on the notion that student teachers needed to know certain uncontroversial routines and techniques, based on common-sense notions of how children learned. Underpinning this training was the idea that the best way of learning to teach was by some sort of apprenticeship, for instance, learning by imitation, by observing model lessons and by developing routines and lessons that could be tried out by the trainee in schools with children and young people.

This 'sitting by Nellie' approach was challenged as training institutions started to aspire to status as higher education institutions, and in particular as their programmes were increasingly validated by universities as Certificates of Education and later as Bachelors of Education. This change was justified in terms of the need to develop teaching as a profession, comparable to other professions. In order to develop academic and professional respectability in this new context, it became necessary to defend teacher training in terms that university validators could understand. This need in part resulted from the persistent scepticism that universities had suffered with respect to the more eclectic disciplines. The 'pure' and theoretical subjects such as philosophy, theology and pure mathematics, have generally had a higher status than the applied subjects such as education, engineering and, more recently, media studies. The university influence led to a period of change for teacher training curricula that encouraged education to redefine itself as a 'subject': that is, a system of knowledge based on one or more disciplines. This change signalled an 'autonomous professional age' (Hargreaves, 1996), where the aspiration was to create an all-graduate profession consisting of knowledgeable individuals equipped to make professional decisions. The disciplines that came to underpin education were those of the emerging social sciences, particularly psychology and sociology, together with philosophy, history and (to a lesser extent) comparative studies. This discipline base for education may have emerged, less from a systematic analysis of the nature of the teacher's role, than as a result of a power struggle between the most credible of the various claims of disciplines whose concerns clearly encompassed educational matters. Had the autonomous professional age emerged at a later date, the dominant discipline base for teacher education might well have included cultural studies and management studies.

The emergence of a discipline base for education as a mechanism for achieving academic and professional status had a number of consequences, some of which might be viewed as less fortunate than others. Research into teaching and learning gained recognition by conforming to traditional criteria for academic research, but these criteria were largely imported from the sciences without adequate re-contextualisation. Thus reliability was often valued more than relevance, and validity was discussed in terms of experimental and quasi-experimental research design, rather than of applicability of findings or content validity. Educationalists in training institutions were seen as experts in their subjects, rather than as experts in teaching. Thus, it became possible for trainers who had no qualifications in or experience of teaching a particular age phase to be employed on initial teacher education and professional development programmes for that age phase. Indeed, professional development was largely seen as something provided by experts within institutions (usually in the form of 'courses') for the individual professional, rather than (say) as something jointly conceived and developed on behalf of schools and colleges themselves. Discipline-based teacher education may be understood as conforming to a 'technical rationality' (Schön, 1983) which treated professional action as the application of theory to practice, denying the indeterminate, 'messy', value-laden nature of professional practice and the nature of knowledge-in-action or 'artistry' (much of it spontaneous and tacit). Schön's work (for example, Schön, 1983, 1987) has been very influential amongst those who seek to develop professional education and in many different fields there have been conscious attempts to move beyond a 'technocratic' model (see Bines and Watson, 1992).

Reflection

To what extent do you think that:
a) the status of teaching as a profession
b) the status of educational research
have been affected by the move away from teacher education based on 'disciplines'?

There were also some benefits from the development of a discipline base for education. Firstly, it encouraged the development of a healthy critique of 'common-sense' ideas about teaching, learning the curriculum and assessment. Secondly, the search for evidence about their effects challenged many taken-for-granted educational practices in schools. Thirdly, it enabled a body of theory to develop that could inform practice in schools (and to a lesser extent, colleges) which would also finally inform and challenge practices in training institutions.

Without 'disciplined' thinking and research in higher education institutions about the difficulties that teachers and students were finding in applying theory, later developments might not have been possible. Such developments include the improvement of practice through action or practitioner research models, the notions of theory emerging from the analysis of practice and, most recently, the development of the reflective practitioner model. What these have in common is a recognition of the importance of (and indeed a respect for) the professional knowledge of the teacher. There is also recognition that this knowledge could be developed and shared through a process of systematic and cyclical analysis that might do justice to the complexity of classrooms, schools and colleges. Practice and the effects of practice are abiding interests: indeed, there is often an explicit commitment to the improvement of practice in such models.

These approaches have led to a number of real advances in our understanding of how teaching and learning works and how it may be developed. Most importantly, the role of the whole context of child, student and teacher learning and development is becoming better understood. This context includes that of the institution as a whole. Such understanding has led to a more collegiate model of professional development. Schools and colleges become genuine partners in the process of developing and delivering the training for the next generation of teachers and in programmes of professional development for experienced teachers.

Enquiry task

What model of initial teacher training have you experienced/are you experiencing? Discuss its content and approach with a colleague.
Between you:
- list its advantages and disadvantages;
- decide what sort of in-service education or training might help you to build on its strengths or remedy its deficiencies.

In the UK during the 1990s, developments in teacher education were overlaid by a series of political decisions that were often reactive to a context that was no longer relevant. For instance, during the early 1990s, politicians sought to eliminate theory from teacher preparation programmes, in the mistaken view that such theory was based on a sterile and decontextualised study of the disciplines of education (see, for instance, Lawlor, 1990). Other decisions derived from a misunderstanding of the source of some of the ideas within teacher education programmes. For instance, there were political attacks on the emphasis within such programmes on the effects of class, gender and ethnicity: these came from people who seemed to be under the impression that a concern with such issues must be based on a narrow and ideological outlook, rather than on evidence of the lived experience of learners and teachers (Hill, 1991). Worries about such course content led to increased regulation, much of it aimed at making the initial teacher training more curriculum and school-centred. It is interesting to note that regulation has increased at the same time as there has been publicity about the under-achievement of certain sections of the community: for instance boys, members of certain ethnic groups and the 'bottom' 40 per cent of children.

The attempt to move the teacher training agenda away from any understanding of theory threatened to draw what Hargreaves terms the 'collegiate professional age' of teaching to an end and to introduce a 'post-professional age'. In this age, teacher training curricula, both for initial and continuous professional development, would become increasingly prescribed by central government, rather than by professional interests. Standards of training are increasingly restricted to skills and behaviours that are easily assessed and observed (Wilkins, 1996). In such a world, regulations demand that students are largely trained 'on-the-job' and employer-based training aimed at the development of observable competencies, with minimal or no higher education content, becomes acceptable. Teaching is viewed as a simple and unproblematic matter (this is possible if one rejects theory – theory exists to ask the difficult questions and to require evidenced answers); there is no need for experts of any kind (subject or process), since practice can be developed and assessed purely through the process of doing; and there is no required knowledge about teaching (such knowledge is theory) beyond sets of measurable performances.

Fortunately, this is not the whole story. As a practising teacher, you can play your part in mitigating what you might consider to be the worst aspects of policy (such as its divorce from any notion of professional knowledge) and take advantage of what you might decide are the best (for instance, schools' close involvement in partnership for training). You may be able to identify a number of factors suggesting that schools and teachers are not allowing such a

Reflection

What kind of training might encourage more people to come into the profession?

What kind of in-service development might lead to better teacher retention?

depressing picture for teacher education to prevail. Firstly, you may be willing to work with colleagues to preserve hard won partnerships with higher education institutions and you may wish to help to develop new ways in which they can enrich your own and your colleagues' practice. Secondly, as a reflective practitioner, you will wish to develop a respect for evidence within your context. There is reason to think that this respect is comparatively widespread, so you need not feel isolated (Menter and Whitehead, 1995). Her Majesty's Inspectorate (who, after all, are largely drawn from the ranks of successful teachers), along with teachers and other educationalists have noted difficulties within largely school-based courses, such as the loss to quality that the lack of contact with subject and process specialists represents (see for instance HMI, 1991; OFSTED, 1993; 1995; and 1997). This does not mean that there is no place for school-centred development. Such development has been found to be an essential element in the school effectiveness movement (Sammons, Hillman and Mortimore, 1995). However, we are suggesting that professional development (whether at initial or post-experience level) that relies wholly on the resources within particular schools may be successful in the early stages, but may develop into an inward looking, self referring system.

Professional knowledge and teacher education

The nature of professional knowledge has arisen several times in the discussion so far, and in this section we give the matter some brief consideration. 'The knowledge' is the colloquial name for the London taxi-driver's memorisation of streets and routes, tested in an examination before he or she is licensed to practise. Here the boundaries of the knowledge in question are clear in a literal sense. They are not so clear in most professions. Even so, most professions have traditionally been defined by 'a body of knowledge' more than by any of the other attributes that were mentioned earlier in this chapter. This begs the question as to what kind of knowledge we are talking about.

One particularly useful discussion, providing the beginnings of a map of the different kinds of knowledge involved in professional activity, is supplied by Eraut (1994). There is only space for a brief indication here, but Eraut's categories may be illustrated with direct reference to teaching. He begins by outlining *propositional knowledge*, which includes theories and concepts drawn from academic disciplines as well as other kinds of generalisation and principles that are widely known in a field. In relation to teaching, examples of this knowledge would include: a theory of the cyclical nature of experiential learning; propositions from pyschological research into memory, such as demonstrating a probability that meaningful material is remembered better than other material; a theory about the relationship between truancy and crime; or more simply a widespread use of a concept such as 'under-achievement' around which there is some common meaning. All these examples of knowledge could influence the actions of the teacher on a day-to-day basis. Eraut is at pains to point out that it is never a question of simply 'applying' knowledge, but that other processes (such as interpretation and association) are always important as well. Propositional knowledge is usually (but not always) written down, or 'codified'.

But other types of knowledge are at stake when we act professionally. Some of our knowledge takes the form of *impressions* and *interpretations of experience*. Here the focus is on the myriad of experiences the teacher meets – even a single day is packed with new experiences, some of which come to be reflected upon, but most of which remain at the level of impressionistic data. These impressions are likely to be crucial in the making of decisions, especially as we all tend to seek out order and certainty when we construct our internal models of the social world. The result may be broadly positive or negative for the parties involved. A negative example might include where a teacher notices aspects of the personal appearance of students and relates these to other impressions about commitment to learning. The impressions and their interpretation may be shared in the staffroom with a colleague who might well be in some agreement, even if what is being said would not stand up to rational argument or is unsupported by evidence. Impressions may also be ignored if they produce uncomfortable questions, or, conversely, they may be used as a source of experiential learning if we subject them to detailed reflection and build new understandings, perhaps in the form of personal propositional knowledge.

Another category in Eraut's map is *process knowledge*. This refers to knowing *how* to do something. Attempts to codify this type of knowledge do not tend to go very far (as many people find when they begin to assemble flat-packed furniture in accordance with 'simple' instructions). Eraut samples a series of processes typical in professional action, subdividing process knowledge into *acquiring information*, *skilled behaviour*, *deliberative processes*, *giving information* and *directing and controlling one's own behaviour*, discussing each one in turn. In terms of the contribution that this type of knowledge makes to the work of the teacher, we might suggest an example here. Beginning teachers are likely to have come across literature dealing with the use of questions to learners in lessons, or at least distinctions between open and closed questions. However, familiarity with this literature will only take them so far in learning to use questions effectively in the classroom. Hopefully, their early careful deliberation gives way to decisions and actions that are 'deliberate' (in the sense of being intended) yet so rapid that it is difficult to call them decisions at all: they become part of the teacher's set of routines. This example illustrates nicely how *propositions* about the use of questions in the classroom are a necessary but by no means sufficient condition for acquiring the process knowledge underpinning effective use of questions. Beginning teachers often feel (and sometimes say) 'if only someone would *tell* me what to do, I would do it'. Though understandable, this statement is already too simple an analysis for something as apparently straightforward as assembling flat-packed furniture. Where there are large areas of professional action based on process knowledge its limitations are abundantly clear.

However, we need a word of warning here. This is a world in which professional practice does not stand still, and a constant dilemma for most professionals is that their process knowledge has an in-built tendency to become less efficient, compounded by the fact that it is tacit, intuitive and therefore difficult to bring out into the open and subject to scrutiny (see Eraut, 1994, pp. 111–12). This suggests a need for structures and opportunities that will foster reflective, practitioner-focused growth and development.

This brief discussion of the nature of professional knowledge has suggested that it is a complex mixture of at least three elements (*propositional knowledge*; *impressions and interpretations*; *process knowledge*). One implication of this is that the model of the newly qualified teacher put forward by the government and the Teacher Training Agency during the 1990s was based on a theory of knowledge about teaching which was closer to a 'craft' idea than it was to a 'professional' one. There was an assumption that lists of competencies, which by definition describe the performance outcomes of training, are sufficient indicators of professional capability. Such a teacher would be competent in at least four main areas: they would have demonstrated knowledge of at least one specialist subject and the ability to apply that knowledge within teaching; they would be able to manage a class and organise learning; they would be able to assess and record pupils' progress and report on it to parents; and they would have demonstrated an ability to recognise their own further professional development needs.

This approach to measuring professional capability can be seen as an attempt to find a plausible solution to a very old problem. Since the time of the ancient Greeks, a distinction has been drawn between technical knowledge and practical knowledge. Technical knowledge can be written down or codified into formulae, whilst practical knowledge is usually impossible to express in this way. Playing a musical instrument illustrates the difference very well, in that only part of the knowledge in the performance is derived from a musical score: the part that really makes a difference to the quality of the performance is likely to be the part that is beyond technical description and which will have been refined through practice, experience and reflection. Similarly, a great deal of the knowledge of something as complex as teaching will be beyond the technical realm (see Eraut, 1994 for a detailed discussion of the implications of this and related distinctions). Competence measurement appears to resolve this problem by cutting to the chase, by taking practice and 'doing things' as its central or exclusive concern. However, the resolution is something of an illusion, because a list of competencies is, unavoidably, a technical knowledge prescription in its own right.

The notion of competence also features in many first and second level programmes of training for teachers in further and adult education, though here the categories are a little different and reflect some of the commercial concerns of the sector. There tends to be less emphasis on subject knowledge (perhaps because there is already great emphasis laid on this in staff appointment processes), and more emphasis on such matters as student recruitment and entitlement, learners' needs, the management of learning, working in teams, institutional administration and marketing. But whatever elements are included in the list of competencies, the question remains as to whether or not they allow an appropriate model for a professional training. In many cases, higher education institutions and their partners have treated the prescribed lists as necessary but not sufficient summaries of professional capability, managing to find opportunities to continue to attend to areas of professional learning which go beyond the requirements. These areas include such matters as the moral and value dimensions which we would want to insist are part and parcel of the professional teacher's concerns.

Extending notions of professional competence

We see the professional teacher as having certain characteristics in addition to those which tend to become specified as competencies. In particular, such a teacher would have:

- a concern for social justice and equality of opportunity;
- an awareness of some of the longer-term effects and implications of their work with young people, both within and beyond the immediate subject they teach;
- a commitment to the maintenance of pupils' and students' morale;
- a real liking and respect for children and students;
- the ability to communicate this liking and respect; and
- high aspirations and expectations of students, colleagues and themselves.

We would argue that commitment is central to the business of being a professional teacher. If this is the case and if the training of teachers is to be seen as a professional training, it ought to focus on wider issues such as political awareness, rather than being merely task orientated, concentrating solely on the job of teaching and targeted learning. We are not suggesting that you should not seek to develop your practical skills through training programmes, whether at initial level or through programmes of continuing professional development: but rather you may need to focus on practical knowledge and values as well as practical know-how. This implies a role for reflection: the evaluation of practice, based on data, leading to a constructive critique. This in turn implies that you might look for training programmes that develop a range of research skills and enquiry as essential tools for continuing improvement in the match between educational values and practice.

There is a debate as to whether teacher training should encourage students to look for commonalities amongst learners or to focus on individuals. The argument is that there may have been too much focus on individualism in the past. The professional needs the tools to recognise the dilemmas inherent in decisions about whole class versus individual teaching and assessment and the problems inherent in managing differentiated learning. Teacher accreditation requirements mean that student teachers within the secondary age phase must be equipped to make very detailed assessments of all aspects of students' learning. There has been little real debate about these kinds of detailed and individualised records: how useful they are; the proportion of the records that actually inform planning; and whether this is the best use of teacher time, when the pressure on teachers is to engage in whole class or group activity and there is little value accorded to an individualised curriculum.

One of the central messages of this book is that the task of teaching is delicate, sensitive and difficult, but also very important. It is for this reason that we believe that a competence-based 'know-how' training is inadequate. We are suggesting that you may need to develop skills of analysis and reflection in order to acquire 'case-knowledge' derived from your practice and from reports of research and practice, so as to inform situational decision making. Such reports have from time to time been derided as 'mere theory' by those who have not thought deeply about the task of teaching, but accounts like these can help you to access some of the accumulated wisdom and knowledge generated by those who have spent much time studying and thinking about the task of teaching and learning. Without such knowledge, you may lack the analytic tools for meaningful self-assessment and the assessment of the wealth of evidence available within the system.

Practical knowledge of this kind will offer you many opportunities for limited generalisation where you find parallels across time or space or between the difficulties others have faced – or you have faced before – and those currently of concern to you. However, as a reflective practitioner, you will also be concerned to develop skills to diagnose the particular needs of your students as a group and as individuals, and to assess the worthwhile nature of tasks and activities. These skills require a knowledge base if interpretations are to be accurate. For instance, teachers need information about normal expectations, in order to make base-line assessments and to set targets for improvement. Some of this sort of information takes the form of codified technical knowledge, for example analyses of examination results by gender. Clearly, competence is not enough:

you need a variety of thinking skills and the willingness to use them, and it is important to accept that there will be large areas of professional practice that are only predictable in general terms.

In a number of places in this book we have also argued that teaching is a collaborative activity. This implies that professional training should include those skills and qualities that make for responsible team working: for instance, time management skills, a respect for others, a strong ethical code and inter-personal skills.

Patterns of career

In one sense there are as many varieties of teaching career as there are teachers. Newly qualified teachers in schools often take on a curriculum responsibility after a year or two in post. Promotion will depend on personal ambition, the capacities demonstrated, the type and quality of relationships with colleagues, and sometimes on whether a teacher is in a position to move around the country to pursue opportunities. In further education colleges, with a much higher proportion of staff on part-time and short-term contracts than in schools, the full-time teacher can find themselves taking on quite major responsibilities early in their career. In both settings there has been discussion about the way that the best teachers can find themselves 'promoted out of the classroom', and concern about this has led to specific initiatives in the case of schools.

Apart from these general observations, there are other patterns worth noting. In recent years many writers have analysed the extent to which *gender* is significant in the teaching profession. The following extract comes from a very well researched study of the work of secondary school teachers, published in 1994 (24 years after the Equal Pay Act and 19 years after the Sex Discrimination Act):

> ❝ ... the data we have presented indicate that female teachers in the schools were at a disadvantage by comparison with their male colleagues. They taught the larger classes more, and the smaller classes less, than men; they clustered more on the lower, and less on the higher, salary levels than men; and more women than men were on fixed-term contracts. There is no self-evident explanation or justification for this state of affairs. The women worked as long hours

as men and spent more time on in-service training at weekends. Furthermore, there was no difference in 'conscientiousness' between men and women.   (Campbell and Neill, 1994, p. 153)

Campbell and Neill point out that a great deal (though not all) of the variation in salary status is accounted for by length of service, so career breaks can be taken to be the critical factor here.

For some people a teaching career is one of several careers, or something that is not necessarily continuous over an adult working life. Supply teaching is a route into, or back into, the profession for many teachers in schools. It can be very demanding, especially where circumstances have led a group of students to resent the absence of a regular teacher, but many schools build up a pool of regular supply teachers who become known and accepted as part of the staffing of the school by teachers and students alike. Supply teaching demands reliability, versatility and flexibility and the ability to form good relationships relatively quickly in new surroundings. Some teachers find they like the relative distance they can maintain from a school's internal processes and find this gives them a form of autonomy. However, for others these things are important sources of professional identity, and they miss the certainty that comes with continuity or the chance to become central to an organisation's decision making or management. In further education colleges, part-time work is very common and is often combined with other employment. Increasingly, staff are recruited through specialist agencies.

Short-term contracts are another variant in the patterns of a teaching career. Some would see it as an advantage over supply teaching in that the teacher knows they will be in one place for a period of time. Maternity leave for a regular class teacher is a common source of short-term contracts. It is important to be sensitive to the fact that even though long periods of time are usually involved, the class is likely to be working to an established scheme of work and opportunities for major reinterpretations of syllabus pace or content are likely to be limited.

Teachers choose to work part-time for a variety of reasons, including being a parent with young children, running a home or a small business or studying for a qualification of some kind. In further education colleges teachers can be found working to a wide range of contracts, with part-timers doing as little as two hours per week in a subject which relates to the skills and knowledge of a job they do themselves for the rest of the week. In schools, very small part-time contracts are rare: part-time posts are usually expressed as a fraction of a full-time post, for example 0.5 or 0.75. However, the large number of factors that have to be taken into account when drawing up a school timetable mean that a 0.5 contract will hardly ever translate into a teacher working from, say, Monday morning to Wednesday lunchtime in the school week. The picture is often further complicated where schools operate on a two-week timetable. The part-time teacher can find themselves making many more journeys to work than they at first anticipated and, once they are there, that they are expected (and need) to become involved in a range of activities that are much the same as those expected of their full-time colleagues. These include such things as joint planning and preparation, pastoral responsibilities, parents' evenings, departmental meetings and other staff meetings. A balance has to be found which enables participation in the organisation and being informed whilst avoiding the clearly exploitative situation of doing a full-time job on part-time pay. Managing this situation requires patience and well-developed inter-personal skills, and a confidence based on reliable self-knowledge about the size and scope of one's contribution to the work of the school.

Further professional development

Further professional development may be viewed from at least three angles. The first is to begin with the needs of the individual, whilst the second begins with the needs of the school or college. The third, (which at present applies much more in professions other than teaching) is to view further development as arising from the needs of the profession itself in relation to its responsibilities to clients. In nursing or civil engineering, for example, there are *requirements* to undertake professional updating.

All three views are valid starting-points, though perhaps they are best seen as three sides of one triangle because they are so interrelated. In this section we will explore some examples of further professional development and comment on some of the possible outcomes for both individuals and organisations.

Case study

Sarah has just begun working in a new post as a head of English and drama at a large comprehensive school on the outskirts of Manchester. She is a very experienced teacher who has taught Shakespeare throughout the 11–18 age-range and has been involved in school productions of Shakespeare plays for many years. When her school received publicity about the Prince of Wales' Shakespeare Summer School, she decided to apply. Demand for places far outstrips supply, so she was very pleased indeed to be selected. The summer school is run at Stratford-upon-Avon by the education department of the Royal Shakespeare Company during a week in August. It is an opportunity for practising teachers to develop their own knowledge and to learn new ways of teaching Shakespeare to students of all ages and abilities.

During the week participants watch all the current productions on in the Main House and the Swan; there are drama workshops run by actors from the company; discussions with directors; lectures from members of the education department, the Shakespeare Institute and others such as the Royal Shakespeare Company's Literary Manager. In addition to all this, there is a backstage tour, sessions with stage crew, costume makers, electricians, set designers and so on.

Sarah hoped to get two main things from her attendance on the summer school: personal development in her own knowledge and understanding of Shakespeare plus ideas for a production of *Twelfth Night*, which she was directing in her school in the Autumn term. It was her view, at the end of the week, that both these targets had been met. She found the standard of discussion throughout the course had been very high, all the activities were well-thought-out and the people presenting or leading workshops were well-prepared. The practical sessions had given her ideas for how to help the pupils interpret the text and to understand characters. She also enjoyed opportunities for creative work in groups where participants could begin to apply some of what they had learned.

There are many factors that influence how effective a school or college is in raising its students' level of achievement. One of the most important of these is the quality of the professional leadership that is offered at all levels. Ideally, such leadership is both skilled and knowledgeable. This skill and knowledge should be applicable to the local situation, but also contextualised in a wider body of knowledge. This implies that professional training is necessary for educational leaders, as well as the trainee and classroom teacher. This leadership can occur quite early in a teacher's career and continue at various levels: module, project, subject or course leadership and subject co-ordination as well as departmental or institutional level. Each involves some expertise that may be developed through a variety of continuing professional development routes.

In making this statement, we are implying that successful schools and colleges are likely to be learning communities in a full-blown sense, providing training and development for all staff. In such places, learning is for all those in the institution, not just the students (Sammons et al., 1995; Clark, 1995). Working in such a setting, the professional will see their development both in terms of their own professional needs and in terms of the needs and interests of the institution as a whole. Furthermore, if teaching is a collegiate activity, the professional development that supports it should (at least to some extent) be collegiate also. We are suggesting that everyone has something to offer in this process: for instance, the student or beginning teacher, in asking questions and seeking clarification, is encouraging their mentor or experienced colleague to articulate principles of teaching and learning. In doing so, the mentor is likely to think through some of their own taken-for-granted assumptions and practices. Their own understanding or 'theory of teaching' is likely to be adjusted or confirmed as a result.

Ideally, the initial training of teachers, the support of newly qualified teachers, the professional development of the expert teacher and the management training of curriculum and institutional leaders should all be parts of an integrated process. The full development of each of the professionals and professional roles within an institution depends (at least in part) upon this integration. In the right conditions, the experienced teacher is likely to find the opportunity to work with student teachers or newly qualified teachers to be a welcome and rewarding one, since it will constitute an important source for their own professional development and will generate new understandings about the wider organisation.

Case study

A secondary school teacher started her career with a degree and a PGCE qualification. During her PGCE she developed a range of practice skills, planning, evaluation, class management and so on.

In her first post, as an RE teacher, she also became a form tutor for a group of year 9 children, several of whom came from ethnic minority groups. She found her knowledge of culture and religions developed by her initial degree and her PGCE useful in this context, but felt unable to provide the right kind of help to students whose first language was not English. The teacher became interested in English across the curriculum and the ways that teachers of all subjects might support children's language development. She therefore enrolled on a one year part-time certificated course to develop her knowledge of this area.

After a few years, she started to feel ready for promotion. In order to develop her skills she took a short course, 'preparing for management', run by her local authority. As a result of this programme, she received useful advice from local authority officers about the process of promotion and self-presentation and was successful in her application for the post of Programme Leader for Humanities at a local further education college.

When she actually took up the post, the teacher found that she had a lot to learn. She realised that management of even a small team involved more than 'being supportive' and 'knowing your subject' as she had previously thought. She therefore enrolled on the Further Education Staff College Management Development Diploma, during which she learned about inter-personal skills, staff management, managing resources, marketing and accounting.

Armed with a management qualification and with experience of success in managing a small team the teacher applied for and accepted the post of Programme Area Manager for all GCE A levels when the college was reorganised. She became interested in the process of managing change and decided to 'top' up her diploma to a Masters degree, a process which had by then become easier through the introduction of modular courses in her nearest university's department of education.

During the twenty years of her career to date, this teacher has undertaken four major programmes to update her skills and knowledge. Each has made her re-examine some taken-for-granted assumptions and has led to changes in both her values and practice. However, this has not been the sum total of her professional development. In addition she has:

- developed IT skills through a mixture of one day programmes and self-study;
- worked with teams of colleagues within the college on a variety of issues such as ensuring inclusivity, introducing key skills and introducing GNVQs;
- run and attended short courses and staff development seminars within the college and locally;
- learned about and developed open learning programmes.

She has found this regular professional development has not only led her to new skills and opportunities, but has also renewed her enjoyment and enthusiasm for the job of teaching. Though it seems paradoxical, the most useful outcome she has found for each successful professional development experience is to start to know a little more about what she does not know and what she needs to know.

Enquiry task

Identify a colleague whose length of experience is approximately the same as your own. Ask them to spend five or ten minutes jotting down answers to the four questions below and arrange to meet with them for half an hour in a few days' time, preferably somewhere away from the demands of work. At this meeting compare your own answers to theirs:
- Identify three strengths and three weaknesses in your knowledge and practice as a teacher.
- Whether or not you currently hold any management responsibilities, identify three strengths and three weaknesses in your knowledge and practice as a manager or potential manager.
- Is a form of appraisal in operation in your organisation? If so, how are the outcomes of the process used?
- Who is responsible for helping you to develop professionally? Do you have ready access to a relevant senior manager or staff development officer with a remit in this area?

References

APPLE, M. and JUNGCK, S. (1991) 'You don't have to be a teacher to teach in this unit: teaching, technology and control in the classroom', in HARGREAVES, A. and FULLAN, M. (eds) *Understanding Teacher Development*, London: Cassell.

BINES, H. and WATSON, D. (1992) *Developing Professional Education*, Milton Keynes: SRHE/Open University Press.

CAMPBELL, R. J. and NEILL, S. R. St. J. (1994) *Secondary Teachers at Work*, London: Routledge.

CLARK, D. (1995) *Schools as Learning Communities: Transforming Education*, London: Cassell.

DfEE (1992) *Circular 9/92: Criteria for Initial Teacher Training (Secondary Phase)*, London: DfEE.

ERAUT, M. (1994) *Developing Professional Knowledge and Competence*, London: Falmer Press.

HARGREAVES, A. (1996) 'Positive change for school success: setting the agenda for the future', *SCETT Annual Conference*, 22–24 November: Rugby.

HILL, D. (1991) *The Charge of the Right Brigade: The Radical Right's Attack on Teacher Education*, London: The Hillcole Group.

HMI (1991) *School-based Initial (Teacher) Training in England and Wales: A Report by Her Majesty's Inspectorate*, London: Her Majesty's Stationery Office.

HMI (1996) *The Teaching of Reading in 45 Inner London Primary Schools: A Report by Her Majesty's Inspectors in Collaboration with the LEAs of Islington, Southwark and Tower Hamlets*, London: OFSTED.

LAWLOR, S. (1990) *Teachers Mistaught: Training in Theories or Education in Subjects*, London: Centre for Policy Studies.

LAWN, M. and OZGA, J. (1988) 'The educational worker? A re-assessment of teachers', in OZGA, J. (ed.) *Schoolwork*, Milton Keynes: Open University Press.

MENTER, I. and WHITEHEAD, J. (1995) *Learning the Lessons: Reform in Initial Teacher Training*, Bristol: National Union of Teachers.

OFSTED (1993) *The New Teacher in Schools: As a Survey by Her Majesty's Inspectorate in England and Wales*, London: HMSO.

OFSTED (1995) *South Bank University Initial Teacher Training: Secondary PGCE by Distance Learning, Her Majesty's Inspectorate in England and Wales*, London: HMSO.

OFSTED (1997) *The Annual Report of Her Majesty' Chief Inspector of Schools*, London: HMSO.

SAMMONS, P., HILLMAN, J. and MORTIMORE, P. (1995) *Key Characteristics of Effective Schools: A Review of School Effectiveness Research*, London: OFSTED and London Institute of Education.

SCHÖN, D. (1983) *The Reflective Practitioner: How Professionals Think in Action*, New York: Basic Books.

SCHÖN, D. (1987) *Educating the Reflective Practitioner: Towards a New Design for Teaching and Learning in the Professions*, San Francisco: Jossey-Bass.

WILKINS, M. (1996) *Initial Teacher Training: The Dialogue of Culture*, London: Falmer Press.

Further reading

The Bines and Watson (1992) and Eraut (1994) (see above for the full references) books give good accounts of what professionalism means for the teacher. The Bines and Watson book is easier to read and more accessible, but Eraut is worth persisting with as a spur to creative thinking about this issue.

Chapter 8

Managing and being managed
Lynne Walker and *John Ryan*

Introduction

Upon appointment the beginning teacher joins a school or college, an organisation which is pursuing specific goals, structured with a formal pattern of authority which in most cases is a hierarchical system topped by a headteacher or principal. One of the key insights which a new teacher can gain about their chosen work is to begin to understand that each workplace has its culture, ethos, tradition, rituals and rules. Another key understanding is that there are many different roles and tasks involved in formal learning that may be understood with reference to important concepts such as management, leadership and bureaucracy. These refer to arrangements, relationships and practices that may or may not support creativity and that permit particular notions of professionality to prevail.

In this chapter we shall consider the formal organisational structures of educational establishments and the ways in which these impact upon the work of teachers and learners. We shall also discuss some theories and models and practices of management currently evident in school and colleges, with the purpose of shedding some light upon how power is generally exercised by those in formal and informal positions of authority, and, importantly, how it is experienced by teachers.

Understanding the ways in which decisions are made and how new teachers can participate in the process is vital in the very dynamic environment in which schools and colleges currently operate. The successful management of change so that it supports creativity in teachers and students, and the professional development of teachers, is very important. We shall examine some of the main aspects of managing change in the latter part of the chapter.

Working in organisations

Handy and Aitken (1986) propose that schools are the same as other organisations. However, there are bound to be difficulties in applying to schools concepts derived from the study of other organisations, especially when such work is largely based upon studies of business and industry. Nevertheless, there are things that are true of all organisations, and, despite their differences, there are also some theoretical ideas that apply to all organisations, be they schools, colleges, hospitals or banks.

One basic definition of organisations is that they are social units that pursue specific goals that they are structured to serve. Clearly, schools and colleges are explicitly formed to achieve certain goals. The question is which goals?

A common defining feature of organisations is that they have internal patterns and structures of authority. In most schools and colleges this is a formal hierarchical system. However, there will also be informal and unofficial authority which results from personal and professional interaction. In the light of the current pace and extent of change in education some schools are also seeking alternative organisational structures in a search for ways to be more able to cope with and respond creatively to the demands of new initiatives. It is this context of change that has seen the emergence of the concept and practice of team approaches to management in education, especially evident in the setting up of the senior management team (SMT).

Models and metaphors

In order to aid the visualisation of concepts of organisational structure and culture, writers such as Handy and Aitken (1986) and Morgan (1997) have utilised models and metaphors.

One of the most common models is that of a 'pyramid' or 'Greek temple', a hierarchical organisation, described as a *role culture* (see

FIG 8.1
Role culture

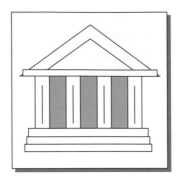

Figure 8.1). At each level of the organisation there are job titles, the fulfilment of which does not depend upon the present occupant: the role itself is paramount. The key organisational idea is that there are roles or jobs connected in an orderly fashion which, when combined, result in the efficient discharge of the work of the organisation. Role cultures are typified by formalised communications, such as detailed procedures and handbooks, and they tend to be managed rather than led. It is common for educational establishments to be structured in this way. People who work in role cultures can find it hard to adapt to change.

In a secondary school the 'Greek temple' may be represented by the headteacher at the top with the deputy headteachers being on the next level down, followed by the heads of faculties and heads of year or house, the heads of subjects and finally the subject teachers and class tutors. There is a clear chain of command which can aid communication, but often the chain is experienced as a conduit of one-way communication in a top-down direction. Most colleges of further education had structures which approximated to this model at some time in the past, though nowadays elements of other models have become more prominent.

Within each level of the hierarchy particular roles and responsibilities provide the official or legitimate power for individual post holders. These roles and responsibilities are frequently reinforced through daily routines, rites and rituals (Johnson and Scholes, 1997). School assemblies are an example of a situation where key staff are displayed in positions of authority. At faculty, departmental and pastoral staff meetings key personnel have dominant and authoritative roles. The way staff are organised and interact on a daily basis provides routines which reinforce the place of members of staff, the students and others associated with the

FIG 8.2
Club culture

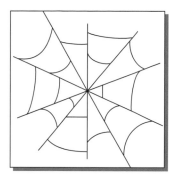

activities of the school. Interview procedures, staff appraisal and competition for promotion are all examples of formal rituals which confirm the hierarchy: these may support or inhibit creative responses and professional action by individuals lower in the 'hierarchy'.

The metaphor of the spider's web is used to describe the *club culture* where the key figure in the organisation sits in the centre surrounded by ever-widening circles of influence (see Figure 8.2). The closer a person is to the spider, the more influence they have. Those furthest from the centre are least likely to see their ideas realised. The model does not represent a permanent hierarchical structure because anyone, at any level, could be close to the central character. The key organisational idea is that the club is there to support the head of the organisation who could be characterised as preferring to do all the work for themselves but who instead resorts to a form of dictatorship, albeit benign. The 'right' people are sought, trust is built and they are expected to respond collectively to crisis. Like the spider and its web, the head and the people in the organisation need each other: they are mutually dependent. A political party is a good example of the club culture. Schools and colleges can operate with such a culture. The model could be representative of a department or faculty or the whole organisation with the central character being the headteacher/principal. If it is, then having access to the headteacher or principal can place an individual in a very strong position to influence decision making.

Within any educational organisation there are likely to be elements of an informal 'club culture' operating, which involves personnel with key roles or responsibilities, that can hinder, influence or direct work independently of the official and formal channels. Educational

FIG 8.3
Task culture

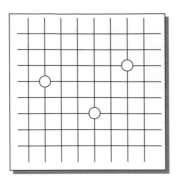

establishments have been described as being 'loosely-coupled' organisations (Weick, 1988) and, amongst other things, this allows several overlapping structures to coexist. Within the establishment there are likely to be shared common goals and a recognised formal management structure, but faculties, departments or year groups often tend to operate with considerable autonomy. The head of faculty/department/year is likely to be the key person at the centre of a web which they have themselves done much to construct. This web can form a 'frame' that constrains or promotes creativity.

A third model is that known as the *task culture*. Here the key organisational idea is that groups or teams of talents and resources are assembled as required in order to work on a specific project, problem or task. Tasks are regarded as being beyond the capacity of one person. Groups are formed to tackle particular tasks, then changed or disbanded once the task has been completed. Such cultures thrive where problem solving is the job of the organisation. Key people are team leaders rather than managers. Such people may have considerable scope for creative action and task groups can provide opportunities for professional development. Many advertising agencies work in this way. (See Figure 8.3.)

The task culture is one where knowledge or capability within a particular area becomes important at a particular time. Thus one person may find themselves at the forefront of change within the organisation because of particular expertise. This happened in many colleges of further education towards the end of the 1980s, when staff who had been involved in the earliest shifts to competence-based assessment often found that the wider organisation needed their help in managing changes that affected the whole college. By the same token, if the National Curriculum was changed so that all subjects

FIG 8.4
Person culture

had to incorporate an historical dimension, a historian within the organisation might find themselves in an important leadership role. The following year the leadership role might switch to another person if, for example, Information Technology was given a higher profile across all subjects.

A fourth organisational culture is the *person culture*. This puts the individual first and harnesses her/him to the task. The key organisational idea is that of the autonomous professional: individual talent must be serviced by minimal organisation. Good examples of such cultures are medical doctors in a general practitioner role, research professors and barristers in chambers. The professionals working in person cultures are fairly autonomous and in general the formal management of the organisation has little control over the professionals. In Figure 8.4 the square represents the organisation as a whole and each star within it represents an individual. Although there may be formal management structures, much common general practice, rules or regulations to be adhered to, and so on, essentially each individual organises their own working practices.

The person culture is likely to exist in addition to the formal structures outlined in the other three cultures. Within an educational establishment each star could represent individual teachers within their classrooms having a certain amount of autonomy despite the complex framework of hierarchical role structures within the institution as a whole. What happens within a classroom is very much determined by the individual teacher. Each teacher will respond to a broad range of issues that include:
■ the subject content;
■ the available resources and accommodation;
■ the student group; and

Reflection

Think about your own organisation in terms of the four models presented above.
- Is your school/college closer to one or another of the models?
- Are there aspects of the organisational culture of your school/college that you would like to see change?

- different approaches to teaching and learning that may be adopted at different times depending on the circumstances.

The person-centred model presents teachers or lecturers as autonomous professionals; individuals sharing some common overall goals and working within a formal management structure, yet exercising control over their day-to-day work. The school or college would be an organisation which encouraged autonomy, its formal structures operating to support the individual and to provide common standards so that student experience is similar throughout the organisation. However, the individual nature of the construction of professional action may not provide the opportunity for the challenging of practices and assumptions that is often the spur to creative thinking and action.

In his study of organisation theory and practice, Gareth Morgan (1997) develops a series of eight descriptive metaphors and challenges the dominant organisational metaphor of the western industrial world, the machine bureaucracy. He invokes new metaphors for organisations (for example as organisms, as brains – the learning organisation – or as cultures). The main idea here is that new perspectives such as these are required in order to transform organisations in creative ways that will enable them to respond to and withstand the profound changes that are now underway, as well as those that await us in the future.

Morgan believes that effective management requires an explicit commitment to forms of organisation that reflect and value individuals' strengths: this would not be rigidly hierarchical and not based upon the classic machine metaphor, but would be one which ensures participation; more than that, it must produce a situation in which there is constant and critical engagement with the possibility that things could be otherwise. It is worth comparing this idea with those presented in Chapter 2 of this volume.

School or college culture

There is also a wide range of other factors for consideration when studying the culture of a school or college as an organisation. Focusing on schools, Brandes and Ginnis (1990) provide useful insights into alternative cultures and organisational structures, with an emphasis upon the desire to create a student-centred environment.

Enquiry task

Listed below are a number of aspects of life in schools and colleges that say something about the culture and ethos of the organisation:

Organisation of teaching
- Is there streaming or setting?
- Is there selection and if so, on what grounds?
- How are resources allocated?
- What policies are in place? Who devised them, and how are they monitored?
- How is student achievement communicated, and to whom?
- Is there collective activity around curriculum development or teaching methods?

Student sub-culture
- Do sporting, musical and other activities have a profile beyond their immediate subject setting? Are they celebrated?
- Is it possible to generalise about students' attitudes to academic and vocational courses and success within these?
- What friendship groups are there?
- What issues are there around gender or ethnicity for students?
- How seriously are student views taken in organisational decision making?

Staffroom culture
- Are there written or unwritten rules about student access to staff outside scheduled lessons?
- Do all staff visit and/or use one staffroom?
- How do staff behave with each other during the times spent together in the staffroom?
- Are there regular patterns in staff conversations?

Gender and ethnicity
- Does the staff and student body reflect the local ethnic composition?
- What proportions of men and women occupy the various management roles?
- Does the school/college make explicit claims in regard to the education or achievements of male and female students? If so, do staff in general share a commitment? Are there pockets of scepticism?

Type of organisation
- If a school, is it Grant Maintained, Voluntary Aided, under the Local Education Authority, or independent?
- Are there strong or weak connections with a religion?
- Which members of the governing body seem to be particularly influential?
- How do league tables impinge on the culture of the organisation?

Try to answer each of the questions above in relation to your own school or college. Ask a colleague to help you do this. Then go through the questions once more, this time thinking about another school or college you know. Make a note of major similarities and differences.

School structures

Schools have traditionally split the work of the organisation into two areas of responsibility: the curriculum and pastoral care, each overseen by a deputy headteacher. Although this helps to spread the workload, particularly at middle management level, it can create conflicting demands upon individuals and suggests that the two areas are distinctive and separate when in reality there are very many overlaps. Students do not on the whole experience their lives split into academic and pastoral matters.

Having two hierarchical structures in operation seems complex enough, but typically there are other structures relating to administration, resources, finance, technical support and maintenance. Although these are often seen as separate from the two structures outlined above, in reality there is again much day-to-day interaction and overlap.

Case study

'Severnside High School' had a headteacher who had been in post for 25 years and she was supported by a deputy headteacher and heads and deputy heads of departments. Much of the general school administration, such as registration and pastoral care, was undertaken on a house basis with every member of staff allocated to work within a particular house. The pastoral network was managed by heads of house who were recipients of salary enhancements but much less than those of heads of department.

When the headteacher retired her successor quickly set about the task of reorganising the whole school management structure. The deputy headteacher role was changed to deputy headteacher i/c curriculum and a new post of deputy headteacher i/c pastoral care was appointed. The house system was maintained for competitive sporting activities but was replaced for administrative and pastoral purposes with a year system. New posts of head of year were appointed, on a salary par with heads of department, to work directly with the deputy headteacher i/c pastoral. The overall result of these changes was to widen the span of control by creating a second tier of line management within the school. It was an opportunity for the new headteacher to appoint like-minded people into important management roles and had some aspects in common with the club culture described above. With some people gaining more power (heads of year) and others seemingly losing it (heads of department), features of the task culture could also be seen. Furthermore, counter-cultures and sub-cultures, which promoted vested/self-interests, became more apparent in such a situation. Not surprisingly, most teachers, who had roles to play in both curriculum and pastoral care within the institution, found this management transition very difficult. Some retreated into their own classroom where they tried to escape much of the micro-political activity and create a person culture for at least some of their time. The overlapping nature of school cultures was clearly visible at Severnside High School. A role culture became the formal and dominant culture, but elements of the others were still recognisable.

The management of educational organisations

In an educational organisation, management is usually associated with formal authority, a designated role or responsibility within an organisation. As Quinlan (1992) puts it, 'a manager is one who has responsibility for the performance of other staff, for learners, and the curriculum'. Many teachers conceive of management as something done *to* them by others further up the hierarchy who are paid more, but in the UK, during the last ten years in particular (post-ERA, 1988) most teachers and lecturers have become managers of learning for their pupils and students *and* have responsibility for the associated curriculum management. It is also very common to find teachers having some kind of management role as a course or team leader. In practice, a continuum of management responsibility is evolving to replace the rather dated concept of managers and those who are managed.

Management and *leadership* are often used as transferable or interchangeable terms. There is, however, no reason to assume that a person in an educational establishment who occupies a management role is necessarily an effective leader. It may be desirable to possess sound leadership capability to be a good manager, but equally it may not always be the case and 'facilitator' ability may suffice.

Leadership is perhaps associated more with having a particular capability rather than formal authority. It is possible to make some clear distinctions between management and leadership, but it is also important to recognise that there is much overlap and in most institutions leaders are often also those with management responsibility.

Leadership styles

Leadership is very much about gaining the support, co-operation and participation of the people with whom you work. It involves motivating others, enabling them to generate creative responses to problems, and striving for desirable goals and changes. Personality traits such as charisma and self-confidence are often recognised in effective leaders, as are skills such as persuasiveness, sensitivity to change and effectiveness in planning and delivering a strategy.

Leadership is often associated with the formal authority which a person has within an organisation, either in post as a manager or as one who has delegated responsibility from management. Having formal authority and power in a leadership role is not the same as being an effective leader since this depends upon a number of factors, not least the traits and skills mentioned above. Informal leadership comes from individuals who do not have formal authority but become leaders because others are attracted to their views or actions and are prepared to support them.

There is a continuum of leadership styles ranging from the very autocratic, who simply issue orders to be obeyed without question, to the very democratic who try to involve others in every aspect of the decision making process. However, the reality of decision making and participation in schools and colleges is heavily influenced by the legal powers and responsibilities held by headteachers, principals and governors, and leads us to the conclusion that these organisations are not democracies.

Fiedler (1977) in describing two very different types of leader, highlights the diverse nature of leadership styles. He describes the *task orientated* leader who places emphasis on the importance of output measures or targets, quantity rather than quality tending to play the major part in planning, often with little regard for people involved in the process. The *relationship orientated* leader, on the other hand, would place emphasis on establishing good personal relationships within the work-place and would be receptive to the views and ideas of others, believing that co-operation is a key factor in achieving success. Relationship oriented leaders are probably supportive, friendly and approachable and concerned for the development and well-being of their subordinates. They are likely to consult and actively seek suggestions, which they would take into account in decision making.

In reality few managers or leaders in education operate with only one style, most have a repertoire of skills that they adapt to each set of circumstances. The manager who aspires to develop as a creative professional and to enable others to discover their own creativity and capacities as professionals, may need to combine the best of both styles, while eschewing the drawbacks of each.

Bureaucracy and delegation

An important aspect of organisations is the administrative process and associated managerial behaviour, often referred to as

Reflection

Bearing in mind both the policy context and the particular situation of a school or college with which you are familiar, consider the following questions.

- What impressions have you formed about the personal leadership style of the head or principal?
- Do you perceive a difference between their words and actions? Are they really open and clear about what is required?
- How would you describe the nature and quality of the relationships the head or principal forms with students, teachers and others in the educational community?
- What are the key elements of their leadership style?

bureaucracy. Much of the theory about organisations, including educational organisations, uses 'bureaucracy' as a blanket term to conceal the messiness, emotion and personal relationships that characterise real life in organisations. Although the term is sometimes used pejoratively, it is important to understand that bureaucracy can be both functional as well as dysfunctional. In this context we are describing not only the blizzard of paper and secretarial tasks faced by teachers, which could be described as institutional housework, but also the actual culture of the organisation. Heavily bureaucratised organisations can be stressful places in which to work since bureaucracy can hinder professional autonomy and creativity. The loyalty of teachers is often to professional standards and the professional role, and not necessarily to the demands of superiors or the organisation.

Teachers in the 1990s have less control over many important decisions than their predecessors. Policy is decided elsewhere and by others, the curriculum is decided by others, and teachers have to implement those decisions. There is a very real conflict for teachers between the professional role of the teacher, authority and bureaucracy. However, schools and colleges can be highly autonomous units, especially at classroom level. We would argue that the role of the classroom teacher/lecturer remains the most powerful position in education. Within most schools and colleges teachers are given opportunities to be involved in the decision making process and are expected to contribute to the organisation through formal committees, subject department or faculty meetings, tutor/year group meetings or curriculum interest groups. The empowerment of teachers and lecturers at all levels in the hierarchy should develop trust and encourage individual professional growth whilst enhancing the likelihood of achieving overall institutional success. Teachers value independence in the classroom but can be indifferent to affairs which do not seem to affect teaching directly. Some teachers are reluctant to participate in decision making, especially when things do not go their way. Others may accept uncritically direction and policy from others, including external agencies.

It is not uncommon in educational establishments to find that a great deal of power and control over day-to-day operations is devolved, with particular individuals and groups empowered to make decisions and take control over many aspects of their work. A head of faculty is likely to have full control over the spending of an allocated budget, deciding which syllabi to follow and which courses to offer. Middle managers, such as heads of department or faculty, are also accountable for their actions to a deputy headteacher or principal. Deciding upon an appropriate action plan for an individual student or a particular class might initially be the responsibility of the individual teacher/lecturer, often in consultation with their head of department/year/faculty. Although accountable to the senior management of the institution, teachers/lecturers have a good deal of autonomy in most of their day-to-day work. Teachers need to operate independently, with autonomy, because they work in an extremely dynamic environment. Teacher empowerment is, therefore, essential for facilitating day-to-day professional decision making.

Increasingly, the issue of empowering students within the classroom is becoming as important as that of empowering the teachers/lecturers within the institution. The context of a particular topic of work is now often negotiated with the students. The research-based nature of much study today and the greater use of team work also means that greater autonomy has to be given to the students. Many teachers believe that if students have more control over their work, motivation is likely to be higher.

At department/year/faculty level a feeling of shared responsibility can lead to greater success and efficiency. Teamwork and wider participation in decision making are often important features of cohesion and success at this level. These groups, however, need to be empowered by the senior management of the institution in the same way as individual teachers are at the classroom level and, increasingly, students are within the classroom. Maintaining control, yet creating the advantageous semi-autonomous working environments outlined above can prove a dilemma for educational managers and teachers alike. There is a desire for staff and students to work as independently as possible, but there is also a responsibility to ensure that their work is carried out effectively and efficiently.

Women and management in education

Education management remains firmly gendered and, as many writers have suggested, women managers are still scarce but also very visible once appointed. According to the Institute of Management only 3 per cent of senior managers in business and industry are women, and although some aspects of the situation in education are similar, things are changing.

The *Times Educational Supplement* (TES, 30 October 1998) reported that in primary schools the work-force is made up of 82 per cent women and 18 per cent men, but in management terms men fare very much better since they fill 45 per cent of primary headships. In the secondary phase things are very different: the work-force is more evenly balanced, with 48 per cent men and 52 per cent women, but in terms of headships 76 per cent are held by men and only 24 per cent by women. It would appear that the situation is changing, albeit slowly, since John Howson (1998) reports in a recent survey that he discovered 44 per cent of new secondary school deputies appointed in 1997 were women, as were 31 per cent of new secondary headteachers. We can justifiably ask what it is that makes the difference regarding the last rung on the promotion ladder. Equal distribution between the genders exists up to the level of the second salary scale responsibility allowance, that is middle management. This is a story of disadvantage and inequality. There *is* discrimination and opposition and there *are* very real barriers to advancement for women. Listed below are some of the probable barriers:

- Interview procedures – the practice of 'cloning', the tendency of individuals, organisations and groups to replicate themselves or others that are close to them, whenever they have the opportunity to do so. Every time someone is to be hired or promoted there are two criteria that come into play. One is competence to do the job; the other is the fit between the individual to be hired and the rest of the staff. This is where the cloning takes place.

- The male domination of headship and the powerful informal networks that are predominantly male. A survey in 1994 by employment consultants InterExec found that men are seven times more likely than women to get a job through personal contacts. Networking is one of the keys to success and women are beginning to make progress in this vital aspect of career development.

- Recruitment patterns – which affect women returners in that they usually have to re-start their careers from the bottom rung. Also, many women move between areas for their partner's promotion, but the reverse is much less common.

■ Ozga and Walker (1995) believe that most conventional education management theory is predicated on ideas from business and industry, it is not part of debates in the social sciences, and does not connect to ideas about power, gender, class, and emergent economic patterns. As a consequence there is no engagement with the heavily gendered nature of the division of labour between managers and managed in the education work-force, nor is there any serious attempt to address issues of power and control in education work. The policy context gives enormous status and responsibility to management, and constructs an edifice of management wisdom and strength sufficient to achieve the transformation of a 'failing school'. The rhetoric may be different, but we are seeing the re-emergence of the headteacher as hero, charged with the mission of school effectiveness.

■ The culture of schools and colleges – it is a cliché to say that men and women are different but when one gender dominates the field of management it is often very difficult indeed to conceive of management in anything other than the conventional way in which it has come to be defined, described and organised. Some women take one look at the current championing of strong leadership in a culture where virtually any admission of difficulty is seen as weakness or failure, and decide they want nothing to do with management. From these assumptions others follow: for example, that women are naturally predisposed to supportive positions or affiliative roles, and that the minority that achieve management status need to adopt masculine modes of behaviour in order to be assimilated and accepted. Studies about the work of women managers in education in North America (for example Shakeshaft, 1989) and current work in the UK, report differences from the masculine convention of management behaviour, including differences in the definition of task, with greater emphasis on cohesiveness and integration, less stress and conflict and the eschewing of anger as a control mechanism, and much more group activity.

The essential point is that most of the material on which education management has drawn in order to construct principles and precepts of action has been based almost exclusively on male experience and on research with men, and has ignored women's experience. Many teachers are aware of the shortcomings of management courses, but embrace expediency in pursuit of career advancement. The management skills identified as necessary for the entrepreneurial financial managers of schools and colleges in the 1990s have produced a growth of qualifications connected to business management ideas and practices.

At the same time, it is arguable that some women seem to have a capacity for self-criticism that can precipitate a crisis of confidence which results in women applying for fewer management posts than their male peers. Men seem to apply for as many jobs as it takes to get them to the level to which they aspire, whereas their female counterparts often decide not to proceed with applications after a small number of unsuccessful attempts.

One can see the emergence of an increasingly masculine management cadre at all levels in education, as women lose opportunities for promotion in dwindling numbers of single-sex schools, and as the focus on efficiency reinforces stereotypical school governor behaviour in selecting 'the best man for the job'. For this reason, we want to conclude this section by suggesting that there is a real need to create a new construct of management in order to force a move away from the rather restricted mode in which it currently operates. Educational establishments would be richer and perhaps more effective if we could liberate male managers from the strictures imposed by current definitions and practice and embrace the virtues and strengths which women often bring, but which are currently undervalued and excluded by male-dominated definitions of management and professionalism.

The management of change

Change is certainly one of the management buzzwords of the 1990s, but it also offers a useful comment on the nature of the lives lived by so many of us; in the words of John F. Kennedy, US President, in 1963, '. . . change is the law of life and those who only look to the past or the present are certain to miss the future'.

Undoubtedly, this is a time of unprecedented change in education both in pace and volume. However, it is important to remember that in the end we cannot become what we want to be by remaining what we are. Existing systems produce existing results and if something new is required, the system must be changed. It can be argued that we live in a non-rational world, that there is no point in lamenting the fact that the system is unreasonable, and no gain to be had in waiting around for it to become more reasonable. So change is endemic, an integral part of modern life, and contending with it and learning from it are central to the development of society but it is constantly under-estimated in terms of how hard it is and how long it takes. The real challenge for both managers and managed is that most change is power coercive, forced upon us by external agents and agencies and it is that which produces antagonism and stress and an aversion to change. Of course, not all change from above is counter-productive, but it is quite common to feel frustrated by the way change is managed by those above us.

Change seldom follows the outcomes of research and the penalty we pay is that much current change is not based upon a body of knowledge; ironically, it is research that tells us that change is often a mix of political dogma and knee-jerk reaction to real needs and is therefore often chaotic and ill-considered. For this reason much change fails ultimately to achieve the ends it was set up to achieve.

Many people make the mistake of assuming that change is a rational activity, undertaken by rational people – generally too little emphasis is placed upon the user of the innovation or change. Ideas about changes are often welcomed but it is the implementation which causes opposition, worry and stress. Change is not just about the creation of new policies and procedures to implement external mandates. It is also about the development of personal strategies by individuals and about their creative response and the ways they seek to influence the impact of structural or cultural or personal change, as much as organisational change. Change is first and foremost about people rather than things.

Placing people at the centre of change management usually requires a creative response in order to rethink existing strategies for planned change. These existing strategies may have served simply to confuse and frustrate because they failed to recognise the dynamic and complex nature of change itself and to take cognisance of the setting in which the change was to take place. Therefore dealing with change does not mean designing increasingly sophisticated reform strategies; these are merely better ways of getting more innovation into the system. Nothing short of what Michael Fullan (1991) calls a 'new mindset' is needed, a different way of thinking about change – a 'paradigm shift'. Such a shift has implications for everyone concerned with management and it is important that at a time when managers are paid to deliver change, they become very skilled at seeing and dealing with its uncertainties.

Education has a crucial role in nurturing within each of us the skills and capacities required to function productively in an increasingly complex and constantly changing world. To undertake this work of making a difference to the lives of individuals requires, on the part of the educator who aspires to professionalism, a personal vision, aim or goal, mastery of professional knowledge and skills, commitment to career-long enquiry and a willingness to pursue personal learning through imagination and collaboration. Thus responsible management is about enabling individuals to become expert at dealing creatively with change as a normal part of their work, a means of coping with the latest shifts in policy and practice, rather than always being reactive. Understanding the process of change, strategies for change and models of change are not only desirable, they are an essential part of the creative professional's toolkit.

Management style, leadership and change

The personal management style of the principle change agent, that is the key person either initiating or charged with managing the change, is of vital importance. The current political and policy context gives enormous status and responsibility to management, and constructs an edifice of management wisdom and strength sufficient to achieve the transformation of a business, an industry, a school, a college, or for that matter, a university.

There is also the whole structure of conventional gendered expectations of management, with which to contend. Managers supposedly behave in particular, well-rehearsed ways; they are purposeful, rational, decisive and technologically competent – the sub-text here being that change is safe in their hands. Women managers are especially vulnerable to criticism when such stereotypical expectations are not met, and perhaps this explains the propensity of some of the vulnerable and highly visible minority of women managers to display a stereotypical managerialism.

Successful management of change requires certain qualities of leadership, as well as the ability to deal or negotiate successfully with vested interests and/or significant individuals. We argue that creativity is also a prerequisite for good management and as a response to change. The status of an individual change agent is crucial: notions of credibility and the status of knowledge all play their part in ensuring success or failure of change. Successful change demands first-class communication in order to reduce uncertainty and gain commitment. Staff attitudes and morale, student attitudes, unclear costs and benefits, uncertainty and anxiety will all impact upon resistance to change or its enthusiastic acceptance. The importance of tradition should not be under-estimated either, since if the ethos of an institution is one which is not conducive to change, the task of implementing innovation is made much more difficult.

It can be argued that *role culture* is still the dominant organisational culture in education. As reflected in a structure, this provides for authoritative power to flow from the top to the bottom of the organisation through its multi-layered hierarchy, deliberately configured to dominate and segment the workforce. The assumptions here are that workers cannot be trusted, work only for instrumental gain, lack creativity, will not take responsibility nor show initiative and will resist change unless they are coerced. The result may well be a kind of self-fulfilling prophecy, in that resisting change becomes one of the few areas in which staff can be truly creative.

The most successful organisations build change up from the bottom, initiating systematic change in individual units and departments. Increasing numbers of staff are enabled to develop ownership of new ways of doing things because they are involved in problem-solving, task-oriented activity, where they are drawn into new informal teams as required, and are offered training and development in order to support their activity. They are able to develop ownership of change because they have an investment in it and thus contribute to the building of the wider organisational vision.

Planning for change

Arguably, managers should be committed to creating conditions in which members of the organisation themselves take responsibility for planning and development. Planning for change should not be an arena for the demonstration of senior management power over departments or individuals, rather a situation in which possibilities and problems may be explored. In many settings this requires a very considerable cultural shift and one that respects the professionalism of staff and includes a belief in their creative capacity. In particular, it requires the use of power to empower others, so that the power relationship is mediated and ameliorated, if not transformed. However, in a climate of uncertainty and insecurity, there is often the desire for conventional (strong) leadership to solve all problems and dissipate all threats. An alienated and demoralised work-force, buffeted by constant policy change, is not readily attracted by power sharing: indeed, the verdict may be that professional responsibility is being shirked by managers – 'You do it, that's what you're paid for'.

Many people in education now agree that we need to create learning organisations – expert at dealing with change as a normal part of their work, not just in relation to the latest policy but as a way of life. Fullan (1991) argues that from inception to incorporation, a major change may take three to five years. It is usually the initiation stage of a change that attracts most enthusiasm and energy, but it is the implementation that requires consistent effort. An awareness of driving and restraining forces and appropriate strategies for dealing with each are as vital as the resources. Training, time and finance are all as important as a consistent clarity of purpose. Implementation is the most important and complex phase of the change process and yet it is the most often neglected. The consequences of this neglect are that the change rarely proceeds to the final stage of incorporation. Incorporation concerns the embedding of the change within an organisation. Resources need to be devoted to review and evaluation, both of which are particularly crucial to the successful adoption and institutionalisation of the change. Change is a moving target – it is rarely one thing accomplished neatly without cost or disruption. Fullan emphasises its complexity and interaction, conceding that we cannot fully anticipate its effects because simple changes may have far-reaching consequences.

We would suggest that there are four levels of change and characterise them in order of ascending difficulty as follows:
- the adoption of new materials, tools, textbooks, new product lines, new services, new information technology. In most cases these are relatively easy to adopt and relatively easy to persuade many to accept.

Reflection

Think about your professional experience of change, make a few notes describing a particular change, and then answer the following questions:

- how did the idea for the change originate? Was it externally imposed or part of an institutional development plan?
- was the change successful? List the factors which you think made it a success or, alternatively, a failure.
- who were the main proponents of the change or the change agents?
- do you think the change was needed? Were there barriers to change and how were they dealt with?
- will the change last?

- the adoption of new knowledge. This is more difficult, since the widening of an individual's knowledge base can be very threatening.
- the adoption of new behaviour, practices or structures. Again, this is difficult.
- the adoption of new beliefs or values. This is very difficult to bring about.

The vast majority of professional development and training is focused upon the first of these and to a lesser extent the second. In reality this will have little impact upon the third and fourth levels of change (behaviour, practices, beliefs and values). People will pretend to deliver new things but will not. They may appear to 'buy in' to the latest change but will remain philosophically committed to their own beliefs and values. The big question is this: is the failure of change due to the implementation of poor ideas, or to the inability to implement good ideas? There is also a need to understand that to change and to improve are two different things. In endeavouring to make sense of the volume and pace of change, in seeking to both prioritise work after wave upon wave of change and to maintain a sense of perspective, we should consider how significant some changes will be in 12 months time. This might serve to help us gain a sense of proportion and to reach an understanding that not everything that is urgent is important.

Conclusion

We are of the view that to develop as creative professionals it is vital that all beginning and relatively new teachers (as well as their more experienced colleagues) have an understanding of the complexity of the organisations within which they work. Even if a teacher has no management aspirations, being effective depends upon insights into the working of all aspects of educational organisations and the challenges faced by those at various levels within it.

Leadership of a whole institution, or part thereof, managing change and organising the structure of the school or college in order to maximise the success of all students, all take place in a complex context. We could have written about the external pressures of inspection, changes in managing budgets, marketing the institution and links with the community, to name a few. However, we have chosen to concentrate on some of the key generic aspects of organisational life which we believe will help the beginning teacher. Managing and being managed are both things that can be carried out more or less creatively. An understanding of the constraints and opportunities presented by these aspects of organisational life is a good place to begin one's thinking.

References

BRANDES, D. and GINNIS, P. (1990) *The Student Centred School*, Oxford: Blackwell.

EDWARDS, S. and LYONS, G. (1996) 'It's grim up North for female high flyers', *Times Educational Supplement*, 10 May 1996.

FIEDLER, F. (1977) *Improving Leadership Effectiveness – The Leader Match Concept*, New York: John Wiley and Sons.

FULLAN, M. G. (1991) *The New Meaning of Educational Change*, London: Cassell.

FULLAN, M. G. (1993) *Change Forces: Probing the Depths of Educational Reform*, London: Falmer Press.

FULLAN, M. G. and HARGREAVES, A. (1992) *What's Worth Fighting For in Your School? – Working Together for Improvement*, Milton Keynes: Open University Press.

HANDY, C. and AITKEN, R. (1986) *Understanding Schools as Organisations*, London: Penguin.

HOWSON, J. (1998) 'Is the glass ceiling beginning to crack?', *Times Educational Supplement*, 30 October 1998.

JOHNSON, G. and SCHOLES, K. (1997) *Exploring Corporate Strategy*, Hemel Hempstead: Prentice Hall.

MORGAN, G. (1997) *Images of Organisation* (2nd Edition), London: Sage.

OZGA, J. (ed.) (1993) *Women in Educational Management*, Milton Keynes: Open University Press.

OZGA, J. and WALKER, L. (1995) 'Women in management. Theory and practice', in LIMERICK, B. and LINGARD, B. (eds) *Gender and Changing Educational Management*, Sydney: ACEA/Edward Arnold.

QUINLAN, K. (1992) 'Professional management development in Cheshire', in FIDLER, B. and COOPER, C. (eds) *Staff Appraisal and Staff Management in Schools and Colleges*, Harlow: Longman.

SHAKESHAFT, C. (1989) *Women in Educational Administration*, London: Sage.

WEICK, K. (1988) *Culture and Power in Educational Organisations*, Milton Keynes: Open University Press.

Further reading

Fullan, M. G. (1993) *Change Forces: Probing the Depths of Educational Reform*, London: Falmer Press.
Written in a clear style which helps make more accessible a number of complex key policy and management issues, Fullan offers alternative views of some of the established ways of considering educational change and suggests ways of dealing with its sometimes chaotic nature.

Fullan, M. G. and Hargreaves, A. (1992) *What's Worth Fighting For in Your School? – Working Together for Improvement*, Milton Keynes: Open University Press.
A favourite of many teachers, this is another accessible and straightforward read, although it does challenge us all to think about improving practice. As the title suggests, the book is about everyday challenges, values, priorities and beliefs of the teacher. It is an empowering read.

Ozga, J. (ed.) (1993) *Women in Educational Management*, Milton Keynes: Open University Press.
Women managers speak for themselves about the trials, challenges and rewards of managing in educational contexts. Very interesting personal accounts which together offer an alternative view of management.

Chapter 9

Quality, equality and stakeholding in education

Kate Ashcroft and *Gillian Blunden*

Introduction

Being a professional has many facets. Among these is a willingness to take responsibility for the long-term, as well as the short-term consequences of your actions, and being dedicated to providing the best possible service for all clients. This responsibility and service ideal is operated in a moral framework. In this chapter, we are suggesting that this moral responsibility applies to those providing an educational service to a variety of groups within education, especially those who have the least power and are most disadvantaged in education.

We suggest that, in a free society, all should have a stake in education, and that it should be of benefit to everyone. This implies that we are putting a premium on inclusivity as a basic principle for professional action. Inclusivity in practice is demanding. It demands skills of analysis, political skills, practical teaching skills and evaluative skills. It also demands particular qualities. Among these are a willingness to seek out the perspectives of people whose experience is very different from your own. Empathy, or 'imagining' yourself into another's shoes is not enough. We recommend that you collect actual evidence of how education is experienced by others, from before the first point of contact to completion (or not) of a programme of study. This evidence should be centred upon the way educational experience is articulated and interpreted by the groups themselves. This implies that it is their voice, rather than your interpretation, that is the most important evidence on which to base professional practice.

The principles underpinning inclusive education

Equality of opportunity is an important issue to the professional. It is about the values that underpin effective practice in management, teaching and learning and professionalism. We cannot see a way of reconciling being a professional in education and a lack of concern for the principles of social justice and fairness that underpins equality of opportunity.

In this chapter, we argue that the basic principle that should underpin the professional practice and analysis of those teaching 14–19-year-olds in relation to equality of opportunity is inclusivity. There are various models of inclusivity, three of which are directly relevant to our concerns. The first relates to the notion that the same provision should be open to all – 'entitlement'. This is one of the ideals that underpinned the development of the National Curriculum in England and Wales during the late 1980s. Only in very exceptional cases was it felt that particular children should be excluded from the National Curriculum. The problem with this idea is the lack of match between provision that is designed for the many and the needs and interests of particular groups. As a professional, you can see this problem as an impediment or as a challenge. For instance, you may feel most comfortable teaching a humanities or English curriculum that focuses particularly on the UK and Europe, but recognise that it is important for all students to learn about the heritage and culture of students whose families might have come from the Caribbean or the Indian subcontinent. As a professional, faced with these circumstances, you may feel that it is important to provide young people from minority ethnic groups with a knowledge about the common (dominant) culture. You might consider the effects that the exclusion of other cultures may have on the attitudes and self-esteem of some of the students and the way that restricting knowledge and awareness to the dominant culture can also limit the horizons of those who come from the majority ethnic group. In these circumstances, you might seek creative ways to include the cultural heritage of a variety of groups, including but not restricted to those represented in the class: say, in discussion of the effects of the Industrial Revolution in Britain on other parts of the world or the role of imperialism in sustaining British culture through accepted definitions of 'high culture' at the expense of older indigenous cultures around the world.

Another model of inclusivity sees exclusion as an act that is perpetrated by the educational and cultural system. In this model, differences in experience and attainment are not 'caused' by the individual, but in their treatment by individuals and organisations that wield power. It requires that professionals should seek out and eliminate intentional or unintentional discrimination within their own practice and attitudes and those of the institution where they work.

The final model that we discuss here is an interactive one. This implies that there are differences in experience and needs between groups and students, but these only become disabling or disadvantageous where they are created by the circumstances, institutions or individuals that students encounter. Thus a person in a wheelchair may have no disability in their well-adapted home, but immediately becomes 'disabled' by a world outside that has been built with the needs of the able-bodied in mind. Much of this 'disability' is completely unnecessary and is a result of institutions and systems assuming that the disability resides in the student, rather than in the educational and physical environment.

This model requires that you, as a professional, investigate barriers to learning that are in your or the institution's control with a view to eliminating them. Such barriers include the match between the curriculum and its speed and mode of delivery and the student's needs and experience, the quality of teaching, resources for learning, physical conditions, staffing and the 'climate' for learning (see Ashcroft and Foreman-Peck, 1994, for more details).

The hidden curriculum

The concept of the hidden curriculum has been discussed and debated by a number of writers (see for example, Gatto, 1992; Halifax, 1986; or Lynch, 1989). It refers to all those aspects of school or college life that contribute to the learning experience of students, but that are not part of the official curriculum. There are a number of aspects of the hidden curriculum that you, as a professional, may wish to influence.

The first aspect is that of management. The way that an institution is managed can teach the student many lessons. It can tell him or her about how members of different groups are (or are not) valued. For instance, if most of those at the lower end of the career ladder are female and most of those in top management positions are male, or if male and female teachers are concentrated within particular subject specialisms, this can send messages to male and female students about the appropriateness of particular career aspirations or subject choices. These messages can limit the opportunities of students of both sexes.

Similarly, students can be quick to perceive power and authority as being hierarchically distributed, with themselves at the bottom, if they find themselves studying in a school or college that has no place for students on a student council, course management committee or academic board of studies. Management in such an institution is likely to disregard the voice of students and not to admit the centrality of the student learning experience to the vision and mission of the school or college.

Other aspects of organisation can have great significance for inclusion or exclusion. The way that admission works can send powerful messages about who is welcome. This can be particularly true for students with disabilities, who can find that the way that they are assessed as suitable for inclusion in mainstream provision (or not), may be seriously disempowering. For instance, during interview, admissions tutors in further education colleges may try to assess whether a disabled student can 'manage' a particular programme of study. Alternatively, they might discuss with the student what adaptations the student feels may be helpful in enabling the student to manage their learning. The second approach may be more likely to lead to a genuine inclusion of the student in the mainstream provision of the college.

The hidden curriculum is perhaps most powerfully expressed in the relationships between people within the institution. We have visited schools where a deputy head in charge of the pastoral system spent more time reprimanding children than counselling or helping them. In other schools, we have seen effective anti-racist, anti-bullying and other policies put into practice. Each of these approaches can send powerful messages to children about appropriate ways of behaving and the extent to which they are valued.

The hidden curriculum is also expressed in terms of absence. Students learn about values by what is excluded as well as what is included. Displays that never include black people or people with disabilities, except as victims (for instance as potential recipients of charity), can be seriously disempowering. The overt curriculum is significant in what it leaves out as well as in what is included. For instance, the curriculum may focus on men as figures in history, on European literature, or on examples in science that relate to the experience of particular groups of students rather than others. Particular subjects may be labelled as more technological than others. For instance, more resources may be put into physical sciences or computer studies, traditionally male subjects, than media studies or business studies, where the sexes may be more evenly represented. This may discourage girls from seeing themselves as technologically competent.

The curriculum, or the way a subject is described or presented, can put up barriers to achievement. There has been much recent evidence that the under-achievement of boys may be partly caused by the curriculum: the way that it is presented may not appeal to their needs and interests (see for instance, OFSTED 1996 and 1998). Similarly, the interests of girls may be marginalised by a teacher who fails to take them into account or investigate them.

Case study

One of the chapter authors, Kate Ashcroft, studied the reason girls and young women were interested in media studies and signed up for such courses in large numbers, when other technology-based subjects recruit a majority of boys and young men. She visited a further education college to discuss the issue with the staff teaching a media studies course that was recruiting a majority of female students.

The course leader emphasised the role of technology in all his publicity. At open days and other events he ensured that equipment was available for potential applicants to 'play with'. He had been successful in persuading the college to undertake a major investment in new equipment and felt that this was a factor in the course's strong recruitment record.

In discussion with the students and from a confidential questionnaire that they filled in, it became evident that few were attracted by the technology. Most felt attracted to the subject because of the opportunities that it presented for self-expression. This attraction mainly took the form of aesthetic or political expression. A number of students were attracted to the subject because it provided a way of understanding the social world more fully. They wanted to understand how society worked and the ways that individuals operated within it. A few had entered the course for vocational reasons, though most were aware of the limited opportunities for work within the media and had primarily chosen the course because of interest. None of the female students mentioned were attracted by the opportunity to work with sophisticated equipment or to acquire information and communication technology skills.

When the students were asked about the skills and knowledge that they had acquired, they tended to focus on knowledge about the media, communication skills and group working. Technological skills did not feature. When asked specifically about what ICT skills they had developed, the students were able to name a wide range.

Discussing these results with the course leader led to various changes. Firstly, he decided that students had been recruited despite, rather than because of, his marketing approach. He therefore decided to change it to appeal more to the potential applicants' interests. He felt that their lack of awareness of their competence in ICT probably led the students to undersell themselves to potential employers, so he decided to 'name' the skills the students were acquiring during their course, and to stress their relevance for the world of work.

Reflection

What assumptions are you making about the needs and interests of students that you teach? Do different groups have different attitudes and interests? How might you find out? What use might you make of this information?

The professional in education needs to recognise the various effects of the hidden curriculum. A teacher who is 'good' in a technical sense may be particularly focused on the classroom, especially on building good and equitable relationships with the students. This is important and useful work, but the professional will wish to go beyond this rather limited view of the teacher's role to take an active part in shaping the institution in order to remove barriers to achievement that are created by systems and action (or the absence of systems and action) and by the attitudes of those within the educational system.

Enabling voices to be heard

When the educational needs of the relatively powerless are being discussed, there is often a tension between various ideologies that underpin different models of provision. These ideologies may be identifiable with different interest groups. Some of these interest groups develop structures and employment opportunities for the individuals within them that would be threatened by alternative ideologies or models put forward by other less powerful stakeholders in the educational process. This can lead to professional interests being given more weight and dominance than those of others. This leads to problems for those who wish to articulate an alternative model of professionalism based on moral and ethical principles, in which the interests of non-professional stakeholders might come to the fore. Below we take the case of special educational need as an example, but the tendency to 'professionalise' the powerless can be true of other groups such as gay or lesbian young people, underachieving boys or members of particular ethnic or social groups.

There is a body of research from the world of special education that demonstrates that, while policies of inclusivity are often accepted, there can be considerable opposition to their implementation in practice from teachers (see for instance, Mousley, Rice and Tregenza, 1993). Sometimes, this resistance comes from a desire to protect professional interests. Mitchell and O'Brien (1994) point to professionalisation as a conservative force that tends to preserve continuity of service. This may lead to protectionism, with undue weight being given to the views and expertise of professionals, and the voice of the actual or potential client of educational services being given less emphasis.

Loxley and Thomas (1997) point to various problems and issues that can affect the implementation of inclusivity. They discuss the way that tensions emerge between the interests of professional and administrative groups and the pressure towards de-professionalisation and devolution of power inherent in inclusion. They see the tensions as resulting from the coexistence of (at least some of) the following tendencies in policy:

- Disjointed incrementalism: inconsistencies between policies that are developed over time.
- Excessive proceduralism: time and effort taken up with administering inclusive policies.
- Centralisation/decentralisation: the general organisation of the system and the location of decision making.
- Democratisation: the openness of the system in terms of decision making and access.
- Imperative of professionalisation: the concern with preserving the continuity of services.

- Resources: the extent that policy decisions are shaped by resource implications.
- Customer centredness: the extent to which services meet the needs of students and their parents.
- Systemic dualism: the extent to which systems have been set up that take disadvantaged groups out of the mainstream educational provision.

Loxley and Thomas' (1997) model of professionalisation seems to us to contradict the one that we are advocating in this book. They are discussing professionalism in terms of protectionism and power, admittedly often disguised as benevolence and the desire to do good. We are seeing professionalism in terms of principled action, even where that action may not be in the best interests of the professional, but would be of benefit to other stakeholders in the education process. This form of professionalism requires a depth of understanding and evidence. Without this, it is easy for the teacher to be blinded by self-interest, or by their own experience, to the interests and experience of others.

It is important to realise that there is unlikely to be one ideal model or set of circumstances for inclusivity. For instance, a decentralised system does not, of itself, mean that inclusive policies are more likely to be implemented. What it means is that there is more local freedom to implement, or to ignore such polices. Paradoxically, a centralised policy and a determination to ensure that it is carried out, accompanied by a system of accountability, can sometimes be useful in the implementation of policies that may mean a devolution of power to the most extreme locality (for instance, individual students and their families). Without the will generated by a centralised system, the devolution of power can be blocked by those who at present control resources and systems at the local level (for instance, schools or local education authorities).

Similarly, democratisation does not necessarily allow all voices to be heard. As Loxley and Thomas (1997) point out, allowing for access or giving power to those other than professionals does not mean that the interests of the least powerful will come to the fore: there will be groups and individuals who are more organised or more articulate, whose voices may be heard more clearly than those of others. Parents and students (even where they belong to a particular group) do not

Reflection

Consider the case of either sexuality, gender or race as issues in education. Whose voices are most commonly heard in policy making? To what extent do these voices seem to you to represent the least powerful members of these groups?

constitute an homogeneous mass with a single view or with equal access to the means to express their view.

Perhaps one condition that is essential to our notion of the professional as part of the process of empowerment for all within education is that of client-centredness. This notion has been drawn from both consumerism and ideas about social justice. This mixed genesis has led to very different interpretations of what client-centredness means in practice. In some models it can mean the provision of choices for at least some clients and their families. The problem arises when these impact upon the choices of others: for instance, where those with transport and power can move their children from (at least apparently) under-achieving schools, thereby leading to a cycle of decline that traps the most disadvantaged children.

In another model, the emphasis is on the voice of the individual and maximising the ability of the student and their family to determine the details of appropriate provision. This second model emphasises integration, choice and information. In the case of special educational needs, this model can promote supporting individuals to benefit from mainstream education and their participation (and/or that of their families) in the decision making process.

What advocacy means in practice

In this section we will be discussing one aspect of the provision for students who are disadvantaged in educational terms, namely that of advocacy. Advocacy is the means by which students and their families are empowered to articulate their own needs and interests and should ensure that these needs and interests are taken seriously when provision and resources are determined.

Advocacy presents a challenge for professionalism. It takes power from the 'expert' and puts it in the hands of clients and their families, who may wish to use it in ways that the professional may not approve or find convenient (see Crombie White, 1997). In addition, the client and their family may have a less developed or sophisticated notion of the obstacles to learning. For instance, as a professional teacher, you may have a clear idea that at least some of the difficulties that a student or group encounters in education may not reside in the students themselves. You may be aware of the operation of institutional discrimination: the role that the school or college can play in producing or exacerbating learning problems or disabilities. Families or clients may focus more or less exclusively on the needs of the individual student, or perhaps, include only factors in their most immediate environment (for instance, their relationship with the individual teacher).

On the other hand, it is likely that the students and their families will have more experience of the difficulties that they have encountered than you can envisage. It may be that they are able to point to barriers to achievement that you, the school or college have never considered. You may be an expert on the learning process and factors that commonly jeopardise the educational experience of certain groups, but the individual is likely to be far more knowledgeable than you about their own experience, needs and interests.

Theoretical basis for the concept of 'institutional discrimination'

Institutional discrimination is a complex phenomenon. It arises within situations that on the face of it appear to meet the criteria for selection or treatment on merit, but in reality put up barriers to progress to specific groups because of an attribute or characteristic which they have in common. Below we give a few examples that will make the point clearly. In the UK, in secondary schools it is common practice to grant study leave to students once the public examination season has begun in April/May. Classes are no longer held for Year 11 students. Instead, they are expected to revise for their examinations away from the school premises. Yet for those students who have inadequate facilities for quiet study at home, including young people accommodated by the local authority in residential homes, this arrangement puts up a further barrier to their chances of educational success (Utting, 1991). As a teacher wishing to act as a creative professional, you might wish to suggest a way round this problem that would remove this institutional barrier for this group of students.

Another example we could examine is one that relates to mothers who teach. In many further education colleges and universities, staff may be timetabled to teach during either the 'twilight' period (5–7 p.m.) or evenings (6–9 p.m.). In schools, staff meetings, staff development events and parents' meetings are often held in the early evening. Whilst many parents who are teachers or lecturers might experience difficulties in making themselves available to work during these periods, certain groups of teachers might find it impossible. For example, breastfeeding mothers of very young babies are physically unable to remain at work. If their baby needs feeding and there is no work-place nursery where the child may be cared for, the mother must return to the child. Such mothers, although committed, loyal and professional teachers in every other respect, might be 'marked down' in the promotion stakes and even subjected to disciplinary action by managers unable to identify the barriers to progress that such rigid and unsympathetic work-load organisation might present.

We are arguing that there are indeed ways in which schools and colleges are organised both administratively and culturally *as organisations* that disadvantage certain groups of students or teachers through no fault of their own. In order to remove such barriers that inhibit progress and attainment, it is first necessary to understand the processes that lead to the structuring and institutionalisation of educational disadvantage. We believe that certain groups of students and staff may have their educational progress held back because they are expected to fulfil all kinds of irrelevant criteria in order to move forward. Where these criteria are so taken-for-granted that they become invisible and their consequences are seen as right and just, they are difficult to challenge and change. Thus, in the first of the two examples given above, the educational under-achievement of accommodated children or young people with difficult home circumstances may be commonplace and attributed to a range of circumstances. The administrative action of cancelling classes, ordering study leave and failing to provide a quiet, supervised working environment in school for revision may pass by wholly unnoticed and yet it may contribute in a direct way to the educational under-achievement of such students. Similarly, a teaching contract that requires staff attendance at hours incompatible with childcare responsibilities is often overlooked in explanations of women's under-achievement and can encourage a focus on women's lack of motivation, lack of commitment and lack of relevant experience at senior level in the work-force (Acker, 1984). Only by challenging our taken-for-granted assumptions about the organisation and culture of educational establishments will we begin to recognise these artificial barriers, challenge them and suggest ways in which they might successfully be overcome (Thomas, 1997).

Dimensions of disadvantage

Similar problems have been addressed successfully as regards the education of girls at both primary and secondary level. In the UK, girls consistently outrank boys in GCSE and A Level grades. The concern now is the under-achievement of boys in schools. Some explanations centre on the institutional factors that prevent boys from recognising education as a 'boy-appropriate' activity, whilst other work has gone on to question the very concept of the 'under-achieving boy' (Raphael Reed, 1998; 1999).

However, at the higher levels of education women are still less successful than men: women are still less likely to achieve promotion to the post of secondary school head or university dean or vice-chancellor. Teaching in schools is still 'a good job for the girls and a good career for the boys'. Some subjects being studied at higher levels are still rigidly segregated by sex. Indeed, there is both an absolute and proportional decline in men on teacher education programmes in universities, especially those specialising in primary school teaching. 'Men's' professions still tend to command higher status and salaries than do 'women's'.

Multiple disadvantage can be experienced when the dimensions of social class and race are added into the equation. For all the expansion of higher and further education throughout the 1980s and 1990s, people from Social Class V remain persistently under-represented in higher education. The success of black students in higher education generally is now well-documented, as the effects of anti-racist policies and programmes and positive strategies to enhance attainment have begun to be felt (Blunden and Shah, 1997). The really persistent factor of overall under-achievement is socio-economic class. No action taken to remedy educational disadvantage can be deemed fully successful until this barrier to achievement has been overcome.

Our experience as teachers has included working to give the educationally disadvantaged second, third, fourth and fifth chances of success. Mostly this has been through further and adult education but we have also explored the barriers to entry to higher education for the training of teachers and the institutional factors that have prevented students from benefiting fully from their programmes of study. It is our experience that a creative approach to teaching and learning that recognises and acknowledges as real the grossly handicapping aspects of socio-economic deprivation, and that offers alternative patterns or modes of study to such students, can empower and enable students to begin to take responsibility for their own lives. The strength that a student draws from a teacher who believes in them, who will not accept second best and who always tries to be impartial, will often be translated into that enhanced self-esteem that lies at the heart of educational success. Sound preparation, good classroom management, enthusiasm and knowledge of the subject matter, coupled with an honest and empathetic approach to the learner are some the hallmarks of the professional teacher whose classes 'will make a difference'. However, as we have argued in the rest of this chapter, this is not enough for the creative professional. There are deeper ethical and social questions and understandings that will need to be addressed, as well as the ability really to listen to the range of voices of those with a legitimate stake in the educational process. Without a sense that only the highest of professional standards will do, teachers in schools and colleges may be unable to do justice to the abilities and aspirations of all their students.

Case study

Matthew was born with cerebral palsy (athetoid spasticity) after a breech delivery starved his brain of oxygen at birth. His physical disabilities were severe. He could not walk, talk, control limb movements or dress himself unaided. He could not hold a pen/pencil or turn the pages of a book.

One of the authors of this chapter, Gillian Blunden, first met Matthew when he had completed his special school education and both he and his parents wanted him to follow a mainstream public examination (GCSE) programme. Educational psychologists had assessed Matthew as having the ability to complete such a programme successfully. He was timetabled into Gillian's mainstream GCSE sociology group and she became his personal tutor.

At first, his involuntary limb movements, his sudden and unexpected vocalisations, and the loud thumps of his specially adapted keyboard used for note-taking had the effect of interrupting the concentration of other students in class. However, very soon his classmates became accustomed to his 'unusual behaviour'. Gillian adapted her teaching strategies to involve him in shared note-taking with a fellow student and more fully in class discussions; and she dictated text into his dictaphone to enable him to listen to it at home, rather than attempt to read the textbook. His timetable was organised so that all his classes were located on the same floor as the disabled toilet. The LEA provided additional grants for travelling to and from class in specially adapted taxis, to pay for a scribe for examinations and specialist careers advice.

Gillian negotiated with the examination board so that he could have double time for each paper and a trained scribe to read the examination questions to him and write down his answers under examination conditions. Eventually, after an extended period of study, Matthew achieved five GCSE passes and one A Level. He transferred to the local Higher Education Institution (HEI), qualified as a social worker and is currently employed in a local authority social services department.

Enquiry task

As a classroom teacher you are likely to believe that it is your responsibility to offer students a learning experience within a learning environment that will challenge each person to perform to the best of their ability. Some students, however, may be persistently disruptive and hold back the progress of others since they require your constant attention.

List some strategies that you might adopt in order to secure an effective learning experience for all the students. Discuss your list with an experienced colleague and add to it.

Ask the students to examine their own motivation for their current mode of behaviour and their own aspirations for the session.
- Try to identify ways in which students will feel able to be included in the learning activities you are introducing.
- Identify learning activities in which students themselves will feel valuable and valued in doing well.

Empowerment

Empowerment is a concept that is related to control. It can involve the powerful relinquishing some aspects of control, in order to enable others to feel and to have some real control over their lives and their environment. This empowerment may start with small things, for instance, over aspects of the curriculum, standards, or timing, in order to develop skills and abilities needed for students to take control over the larger things: for example, over their personal life or vocational direction. Empowerment may also involve providing the opportunity to develop skills and understandings, and access to information, that will enable the individual to have more control over the direction of their education and life. For the person who has reading difficulties, the opportunity to acquire basic literacy skills may represent real empowerment. On the other hand, teachers who use sarcasm and embarrassment as a control method may occasionally be effective in terms of behaviour management, but they are likely be disempowering their students in a variety of ways. The empowering teacher and the empowering learning environment is one where the learning needs come first. Institutional organisation and classroom organisation should work to facilitate a clear articulation of student learning needs and then provide the appropriate resources (human and physical) to enable the student to go about meeting those needs.

In a school situation the student's learning needs are all too often defined by the institution, with the voice of the learner and/or their parents or carers wholly overlooked. Within the classroom the morally and ethically aware teacher should be sensitive to this and resist institutional demands to 'package' children's learning needs to meet institutional needs. For example, where a school has a special unit for children with learning difficulties, there is often considerable pressure on the teacher in the mainstream classroom to identify children whose educational needs might be met through the special unit, simply because there are spaces within it and school resources would go to waste if such spaces were not fully utilised.

In order to be able to empower their students, teachers themselves may need to feel empowered both within their own school and the wider education system. This may be more easily achieved where management is organised so that initiative, commitment and creativity are recognised, celebrated and rewarded. A culture of facilitation, enabling and trust may be fostered amongst colleagues, with clear lines of decision making and accountability. Few people object to decisions being taken with which they disagree, provided that the rationale behind the decision is made explicit and that they are confident the decision is a well-informed one. Frustrations become evident where this is not the case.

Quality, standards and the principles of stakeholding

In this section we look at notions of quality and standards and consider their implications for the professional teacher who sees education as a process for promoting opportunity for their students.

Teachers in schools and colleges may feel that a 'quality industry' has developed that has little to do with what they understand to be quality in education. This may be because various parties with an interest in education are defining quality in different ways.

One definition sees quality as faultlessness or consistency. This is an approach that has been applied to manufacturing as a means of ensuring that a product always meets particular specifications. It is a notion of quality that may have influenced the introduction of the National Curriculum and National Vocational Qualifications. Inspectors of schools and colleges may look at curriculum documents and actual practice to ensure that students are receiving a minimum entitlement to the curriculum. As we mentioned above, this can be based on some idea of equity, but it can lead to students' individual needs becoming lost in a more general set of requirements.

Another definition of quality has the notion of excellence at its heart. It is this definition that has led to the defence of particular 'gold standard' assessments. Examples of these are the traditional GCE Advanced level examination, the Oxbridge model of university education and a belief that the move from traditional academic subjects to vocational and applied subjects represents a dumbing down of the curriculum. This model tends not to be inclusive, but rather to preserve traditional values by ensuring that the barriers to individuals achieving recognition for excellence are in place so only those that can meet a relatively narrow definition of high standards can surmount them.

Another definition of quality relates to value for money. Again the principal motivation for this may not be the expansion of opportunity, but rather that of securing the maximum benefit from public investment in education. Taken to its extreme, it may lead to an education system that caters for the majority, but ignores the needs of minorities, especially those that are expensive to accommodate such as students with learning difficulties and the very able. On the other hand, the notion of value for money has recently been adapted to that of 'value added'. This idea suggests that an educational endeavour should be seen as of good quality where it maximises the growth of individuals or groups from various starting-points. This idea has more in common with the concerns of the professional teacher to help each individual to maximise his or her potential.

The final notion of quality relates to fitness for purpose. In this model, education would be seen as being of good quality when it meets the aims and aspirations of various of the stakeholders in education. This model separates the assessment of quality from that of standards. Thus, it is possible for a course that aspires to relatively low standards (for instance one that develops basic literacy) to be judged to be of better quality than one that aspired to and was successful in reaching higher standards (for instance an Advanced Level course).

In order to understand the discomfort that some teachers feel in dealing with issues of quality, it may be useful to consider the various purposes at which various definitions may be directed. The first one is that of bureaucracy. Today's organisations require management information related to quality to enable decisions to be taken. This is true at national level (for instance, OFSTED scores to determine whether a school should be put into special measures) and at a local level (for instance, completion and pass rates for various examination subjects to enable a headteacher to decide whether any subjects should be dropped from the students' option choices).

Sometimes such information is also required for political purposes. For instance, in the UK, such information is collected in order to create league tables containing various performance indicators. This enables the creation of a quasi-market that requires schools and colleges to pay attention to government objectives in order to compete for students and so to survive. It also enables a form of accountability. Schools and colleges can be called to account for their performance and made to justify their continuing receipt of public money.

Bureaucratic and political notions of quality may not appeal to all teachers. The stakeholders that they serve tend not to be those within the teacher's immediate concerns, such as students and other teachers. The intention is to serve the needs of other groups: taxpayers, politicians, managers, parents and so on. On the other hand, on occasions the interests of the least powerful are also served: for instance, students who receive a better education as a result of a school being put on special measures.

Perhaps the main problem with bureaucratic and political definitions of quality is that they each require simple, generally numerical, information to work. Management and policy decisions can be more easily justified if they consist of apparently 'objective' data. Too much information in too complex a form is hard to handle. The larger and more complex the organisation, the simpler such information must be. At the national level, this leads to data on an individual college or school being reduced to a set of numbers. Teachers within these organisations are aware that their future, and that of the organisation, depends to some extent on these scores, but also that such data do not by any means reflect the reality that teachers confront and create each day.

Another model of quality with which teachers may feel more comfortable is the developmental model. This model is based on self-evaluation, backed up by enquiry into the actuality of teaching. It is based on trust, and the belief that teachers are professionals who have an interest in securing the best quality education for their students and are skilful enough to achieve this and monitor their own performance.

Enquiry task

Discuss the models of quality outlined above with a colleague.

List some of the advantages and disadvantages of each from the point of view of the following stakeholders:
- teachers;
- examining bodies;
- government (local and national);
- students;
- employers;
- society.

Ask some students and some parents how they would define quality in education. What model of quality are they using? Can you fit it into one of the frameworks above? Can you place the focus of their concerns along any of the following continua?

economic benefit	versus	cultural benefit
efficiency	versus	effectiveness
short-term benefit	versus	long-term benefit
developmental purposes	versus	accountability

The notion of *standards* underpins much of the recent rhetoric about education (see Ashcroft and Foreman-Peck, 1995 for more detail). Government, schools, local authorities and colleges are concerned to raise standards, but it is not always clear what is meant by this. Teachers and others who question the basis of the debate may find themselves pilloried for being unconcerned about standards. Unfortunately, this debate has obscured a variety of interpretations of the concept of 'standards'. It can be seen as a technical concept that relates to the reliability and level of assessment. In this model, standards are maintained by ensuring moderation of marking, consistency in interpreting criteria year-on-year and so on. Others may use reference to standards as a means of ensuring compliance with particular policies. Thus 'standards' can be laid down that determine the student learning objectives and outcomes, and through this the curriculum, and even teaching methods. Another model, and perhaps the model with which teachers feel most comfortable, sees the debate about standards as being concerned about raising the aspirations and achievement of most children, especially those who are the most challenging to teach.

The debate about quality and standards, and its resolution, is about power. Teachers have a responsibility to take part in processes that secure the resources and learning environment for their students. We would therefore argue that they should take a full part in the debates and in quality processes if they are not to be parasitic on others who do devote time and energy to those processes. If you take your full part, you can make a small contribution towards ensuring that the interests of the least powerful and least privileged stakeholders in education get their voices heard and are not drowned out by others who wield more power and influence.

The professional responsibilities of the teacher in securing the climate for teaching and learning

Teachers who see their work only in terms of the quality of transactions in the classroom may be doing valuable work, but they are relying on others to create the environment that makes teaching and learning possible. We see it as part of the role of the creative professional to secure good and appropriate classroom conditions and curriculum content so that all their students can take advantage of the education on offer and so that all will feel affirmed and valued. This is a necessary, but insufficient condition for inclusivity and equality of opportunity.

However, what of the wider structural and organisational barriers to achievement? As Ashcroft and Foreman-Peck (1995) point out, this implies that the professional takes an interest in much that occurs outside the classroom. In particular, such a professional is concerned to influence policy and practice. This means that they will take an active part in management, planning and decision making processes, including curriculum leadership, management and committee work. It is in such contexts that the institution is defined and an inclusive ethos created.

In order that such professionals can operate effectively and be confident that their classroom practice and contribution to policy and decision making is valid, they need to collect evidence about the options for action. Such knowledge can come from a variety of sources: from the accumulated knowledge of researchers and others who have studied the subject and as found in the literature; from inservice courses and workshops; from discussion and debate with colleagues; and, possibly most importantly, from evidence collected from students themselves and their families about their needs and the effects of various types of interventions to meet these needs.

References

ACKER, S. (1984) (ed.) *World Yearbook of Education: Women in Education*, London: Kogan Page.

ASHCROFT, K. and FOREMAN-PECK, L. (1994) *Managing Teaching and Learning in Further and Higher Education*, London: Falmer Press.

ASHCROFT, K. and FOREMAN-PECK, L. (1995) *The Lecturer's Guide to Quality and Standards in Colleges and Universities*, London: Falmer Press.

BLUNDEN, G. and SHAH, S. (1997) *Widening Participation in Teacher Education: Issues Relating to Ethnic Minority Students*, Centre for Equality Issues, University of Hertfordshire.

CROMBIE WHITE, R. (1997) *Curriculum Innovation: A Celebration of Classroom Practice*, Buckingham: Open University Press.

GATTO, J. T. (1992) *Dumbing Us Down: The Hidden Curriculum in Compulsory Schooling*, London: New Society Publications.

HALIFAX, G. (1986) 'The hidden curriculum: an overview', in MEIGHAN, R. *A Sociology of Educating*, London: Cassell.

LYNCH, K. (1989) *The Hidden Curriculum: Reproduction in Education, a Reappraisal*, London: Falmer Press.

LOXLEY, A. and THOMAS, G. (1997) 'From inclusive policy to exclusive real world: an international review', *Disability and Society*, **12**, 2, pp. 273–91.

MITCHELL, D. and O'BRIEN, P. (1994) 'Special education in New Zealand', in MAZUREK, K. and WINZER, M. (eds) *Comparative Studies in Special Education*, Gallaudet: Gallaudet Press.

MOUSLEY, J. A., RICE, M. and TREGENZA, K. (1993) 'Integration of students with disabilities into regular schools: policy in use', *Disability, Handicap and Society*, **8**, pp. 59–70.

OFSTED (1996) *The Gender Divide: Performance Differences Between Boys and Girls at School*, London: HMSO.

OFSTED (1998) *Recent Research on Gender and Educational Performance*, London: HMSO.

RAPHAEL REED, L. (1998) ' "Zero tolerance": Gender performance and school failure' in EPSTEIN, D., ELLWOOD, J., HEY, Z. and MAW, J. (eds) *Failing Boys? Issues in Gender and Achievement*, Buckingham: Open University Press.

RAPHAEL REED, L. (1999) 'Troubling boys and disturbing discourses on masculinity and schooling: a feminist exploration of current debates and interventions concerning boys in school', *Gender and Education*, **11**, 1, pp. 93–110.

THOMAS, G. (1997) 'What's the use of theory?', *Harvard Educational Review*, **6**, 7, 1, pp. 75–100.

UTTING, W. (1991) *Children in the Public Care: A Review of Residential Childcare*, London: Department of Health.

Further reading

Ashcroft, K., Bigger, S. and Coates, D. (1996) *Researching into Equal Opportunities in Colleges and Universities*, London: Kogan Page.
This book provides an enquiry-based approach to issues of inclusivity, that generally applies as well to school as to post-compulsory education.

Loxley, A. and Thomas, G. (1997) (see above for full reference).
Provides a good outline of many of the main issues involved in empowerment for people with special educational needs.

Chapter 10

Enquiry and the creative professional
Kate Ashcroft

Introduction

This book is based on a particular notion of reflective practice that the authors feel is appropriate for a creative professional teacher. This model sees teaching as a moral activity, that is based on the development of three basic qualities: open-mindedness, responsibility and wholeheartedness. These ideas were introduced by Dewey (1916) and have been developed by writers and philosophers such as Zeichner (1982) in the USA and Ashcroft and Foreman-Peck (1994 and 1996) in Britain.

Open-mindedness implies that the teacher is eager to seek out and understand alternative viewpoints on an issue. These viewpoints may be those of the various stakeholders in the education process: students, other teachers, parents, funders of education as well as writers and researchers operating in other times and places. This implies that the professional teacher should make efforts to discover these perspectives. To do otherwise might restrict the teacher to a technocratic model. Often this will mean collecting data and evidence as to what the various parties to the educational process think and feel: for instance through 'insider research' where the teacher undertakes a small-scale enquiry into aspects of the teaching situation, or through a critical analysis of the available research and other literature of relevance to the situation.

The second quality that we believe underpins reflective practice is that of responsibility. This implies that the teacher looks at the long-term as well as the short-term consequences of their actions. Again, this implies that the teacher is willing to enquire into the teaching situation, to discover what they actually do, how that is perceived by the other parties to the education process and the effects of their attitudes and behaviour on the learning, attitudes and behaviour of others, especially the student. This quality also implies that this enquiry is informed by reading others' ideas and research findings.

The final quality of reflective practice is that of wholeheartedness. It is this aspect that makes the model of practice an essentially moral one, where the educational endeavour, its actions and effects, should be tested against how well they match the professional's articulated values which may include respect for the dignity of the individual and the promotion of opportunity and social justice. Wholeheartedness implies that the teacher moves away from a utilitarian consideration of 'what works', to look at issues of 'worthwhileness'. This means that professional action must be moral and educationally defensible in its intentions and results. The fully professional teacher may need to undertake actions that are not necessarily in their own best interests: for instance, they may need to act as the whistle-blower when they detect corrupt or hypocritical practice. However, in undertaking such action they should be aware that it may disadvantage individuals or a particular institution. Responsibility means that an individual generally should not act impulsively, even with the best of intent, but rather examine honestly and deeply their motives and as many as they can of the effects (intended and unintended) that might result from a particular course of action. Truly professional action often requires the individual to grapple with dilemmas, where there are advantages and disadvantages that may result from possible alternatives. In making decisions that are defensible in terms of reflective practice, the teacher will need as much information and evidence as is possible, and they will need to have cultivated the habit of self-awareness and awareness of the possibility of self-delusion. Such self-awareness is often a useful by-product of open-minded and responsible enquiry into practice.

It is for these reasons that in this chapter I explore the interrelation between enquiry, research and professional practice, and suggest ways that you can develop as a researcher and reader of research.

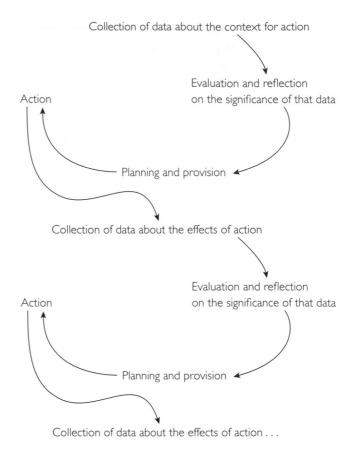

FIG 10.1
Model of reflective action

Evaluation as a feature of professional practice

The notion of reflection as underpinning professional practice implies an evaluation-led activity. This can be conceptualised as shown in Figure 10.1.

This model recognises some of the complexity of the teaching process and puts evaluation at its heart. It implies that the professional does not attempt to teach using a tried-and-tested formula of method and content, but rather undertakes a systematic and critical diagnosis of the context for action. In the light of that context they make plans and prepare for teaching and learning. This preparation will draw on the knowledge gained about the context, but also on knowledge gained from reading, critical evaluation of research conducted by others and the teacher's own experience and training. This planning will inform action, which in turn will be the occasion for more data collection and reflection, leading to analysis and evaluation to inform the planning for the next action.

In using the term 'data' here, I am not implying that this evidence must take a particular form. What counts as evidence will depend upon the purpose for which it is to be used, and the objectives of the teacher. For instance, you may be concerned to promote deeper approaches to learning (see Marton and Saljo, 1984 and Ramsden, 1992 for more on deep and surface approaches to learning). In order to discover the nature of the students' learning, or the effects of your proposed actions, you could use a variety of techniques. For instance, you might discuss their learning at length with a group of students in order to elicit their implicit theories of learning; you might assess the products of their work to see whether there is evidence of understanding and application to their own situations; or you might undertake a questionnaire survey to discover the students' motivations for learning and the strategies they use.

The model of reflection has much in common with the model of action research developed by Stenhouse (1987) and others (for instance, Carr and Kemmis, 1986). It also relates closely to Argyris and Schön's (1974) ideas about the development of theory from practice. The main difference between these ideas and our own is that action research is often focused on a particular problem and involves a cyclical process, and reflective practice is not necessarily problem-based (unless the problem is how to become a more effective teacher) and the process of enquiry does not necessarily conform to a particular model. On the other hand, both require enquiry into practice, both are generous in terms of what may count as evidence and both are centred on the improvement of practice.

Case study

Early in my career, I became very interested in the notion of reflective practice and its implications for students. I felt that the notion might have currency beyond teaching and relate to student learning. I therefore began to read and consider what it might mean to become a 'reflective student'. I became interested in the links between reflective practice for learners, especially those on vocational courses, as expressed in notions of open-mindedness, wholeheartedness and responsibility and outlined by

Zeichner (1982) and theories of deep and surface learning along with ideas from the humanistic tradition, especially those of Rogers (1983).

From this analysis, it appeared to me that student ownership of learning intentions, processes and outcomes might be important and that this could be related to the skills underpinning autonomous and group learning. I was a module leader on a vocational course for a basic module that had around 150 students registered on it. I worked with a staff team of six members to design a programme that would allow the maximum student control of elements such as curriculum, timing, methods and assessment. The students were given responsibility for achieving the main aim of the programme. This was for the group to produce a report that would illuminate the case for and against a broad policy direction related to the subject and vocational area that they were studying. They were required to negotiate a curriculum that would meet this aim, decide on the methods that they might use and undertake peer assessment of the developing and final product. Certain resources were made available to the group. These included:

- a timetabled room;
- a group tutor shared between two seminar groups. The tutor could be booked by a group for a particular session, but otherwise divided his or her time during the module between the two groups, facilitating their work as and when required;
- expert tutors who could be booked for a particular session, provided that they were given a clear brief from the group;
- expert 'witnesses' from the world of work, who were willing to attend on particular days in order to answer questions from a group;
- a visit to a relevant work-place;
- a set of papers and background information;
- a handbook of ideas for making student-led teaching interesting and useful;
- a set of guidelines on the operation of formative and summative peer assessment.

The students were required to work out how they would use these resources to maximise their learning and to achieve the aim of the course. Students were expected to devise strategies to support each other's learning, to monitor their own progress, to ensure reliability and validity of the assessment of the final report.

Since the core team believed in reflective practice for themselves as well as for the students, we designed an ongoing evaluation of the programme from our point of view, from that of the students and from that of colleagues. Each week, this evaluation took a different focus and used a different evidence collection technique. The team shared their findings and interpretation of them with students and with other colleagues. They posted a report each week on the group notice-board, with a space for colleagues and students to add their comments and ideas. This became an organic and growing display of a developing view of the challenging process that we set up for the students and that they had developed for themselves. It revealed the pain and pleasures of autonomous learning, its successes and failures; the difficulties and opportunities presented by group learning; and the ways that this kind of process can lead to profound changes in the attitudes of all involved during the course of the term (see Ashcroft, 1987 for more details).

Evaluation methods and techniques

There are various approaches to evaluation as a preparation for planning and action. Depending upon your objectives, you may decide to go for a rigorous, research-based approach, or, alternatively, for more 'quick and dirty' methods. Whatever approach you take, it is important to understand that all methods have their strengths and weaknesses.

Enquiry task

Try to add to the following list of methods for collecting data on your teaching or students' learning:
    unstructured observation;
    structured observation using a checklist;
    individual interviews;
    group discussion;
    questionnaires;
    tests of students' skills and understanding.

- With a colleague, discuss what each are 'good for' and 'not so good for'. For instance, would you agree that unstructured, fly-on-the-wall observation is good for getting at what you and/or your students actually do, but not so good for getting at what you or they know, think or feel?
- Try out at least one method to discover more about some aspect of your teaching.
- Discuss your results and ways of interpreting them with a colleague.
- What did you learn about your teaching?
- What did you learn about the process of classroom enquiry?

The evaluative techniques I discuss below are suitable for small-scale enquiry. I do not explore methods of statistical analysis, although these can be useful even in small-scale studies. There are computer programmes on the market that can make analysis of numerical or descriptive data relatively simple. You may become inspired to undertake such an analysis. In this case, you may find books such as

Bennett, Higgins and Foreman-Peck (1996) or Cohen and Manion (1985) useful.

There are a variety of evaluation instruments that are available to you. The first, and perhaps the most commonly used in colleges, although perhaps rather underused at present in schools, is the questionnaire. The questionnaire may be open-ended (where you invite comments under a variety of headings), semi-structured (where you invite more limited response, perhaps by asking specific questions) or closed (where you limit possible responses, for instance to yes/no answers or ratings of strength of negative or positive feelings). Questionnaires can be a good way to survey thoughts, feelings and attitudes. They are not so useful for getting at actual behaviour: what people say they do and what they actually do can be very different. You will need to be careful in constructing a questionnaire that will not to seek to lead the respondents to answer in a particular way, and to ensure as far as possible that the respondents will interpret the questions in the way intended.

The advantage of more structured questionnaires is that, in closing the response options that you allow, you make it possible to handle more data and it becomes easier to compare one set of data with another. On the other hand, unstructured or semi-structured questionnaires allow the respondents to express themselves more exactly. Unfortunately, this richness of data makes them difficult to handle. In imposing some sort of order, you may over-simplify the responses in the same way as a more structured questionnaire.

The construction of a questionnaire is a skilled matter. For instance, you will need to ensure that your questions are not ambiguous, that they elicit the appropriate information and that they are expressed simply and in an unthreatening way. (See Ashcroft, Bigger and Coates, 1996, for more details.) Standardised tests can help you get around this problem. They are generally validated professionally and you can compare your findings with those of others. Commonly in the form of questionnaires, they may be useful for assessing particular pieces of learning or attitudes. Generally, they are not good for describing behaviour. For example, so-called aptitude tests predict how well people will perform according to the similarity of their responses to those of people doing a particular job, or ability as measured by fairly crude measures in areas such as problem solving, literacy and numeracy. They may fail to recognise people with talent and flair who could bring something new and important to an organisation simply because they see things in unconventional ways. They may be more useful for teachers in helping them to assess what students have learned and achieved compared with others at the same stage rather than for indicating the capabilities of the students.

Teachers frequently create their own tests or use diagnostic marking of the products of students' learning to assess how successful they have been in promoting knowledge and understanding. These methods can be useful assessment tools, but may need cautious interpretation. Students may underperform relative to their understanding, especially if they have specific problems with expression (for instance, writing or spelling difficulties). On the other hand, they may be able to produce what is expected of them, but lack an understanding of the underpinning processes.

Interviews are good at eliciting responses to issues similar to those in questionnaires. They can be useful if you are concerned about a particular issue or a particular student and wish to discover more about a problem, but, although flexible, they may be too time-consuming for more general evaluation. One way of getting around the problem of time is to conduct group interviews, perhaps drawing upon focus group techniques (see Davies and Headington, 1995, for a description of focus group techniques). Group interviews can give a quick impression of student opinion, but this may be misleading if the session is dominated by particular individuals or a particular faction. The group interview may be most useful as a way for you to check out with the respondents your interpretation of what they are saying and the ways you might categorise their responses. This can then provide categories for other kinds of data collection (for instance, a questionnaire). It is important to remember that there is always a strong possibility in any kind of face-to-face interviewing that the respondent will give the answer that they think you want to hear, especially if there is a power differential in the situation (for instance, if you are the teacher and the respondent is a student). Questionnaires generally allow for confidentiality. There is no hiding place in an interview for socially unacceptable responses, which can be a real problem if you are expecting your students to tell you about the effectiveness of your teaching or their learning.

One creative way round this problem is to pair up with a trusted colleague. If the colleague conducts interviews with your students about your teaching and the ways this has affected the students' learning, and you do the same for your colleague, you may both access more accurate data. It can be hard to tell someone you like the unpalatable opinions of others and you may be tempted to soften the message. You may need to come to an agreement that you will be brutally honest with each other, recognising that this can be painful, and that you may not like your colleague's interpretation of what the students are saying. On the other hand, as a reflective practitioner, you may welcome such painful revelations because they can help you to move forward in your practice.

Scenario analysis is one way of getting people to talk about events, thoughts and feelings. Scenarios can be presented to respondents in the form of pictures, case studies, stories or using some other medium. You could collect responses using a variety of structured and unstructured instruments. Another way of getting at these issues is biographical writing (see for instance, Connolly and Clandinin, 1990; and Cortazzi, 1993). This technique involves you in asking respondents to describe significant events, with more or less guidance from you. As with all forms of stimulated recall, what people tell you, and what they believe about themselves is only one version of the truth. While biography can tell you about people's perceptions, it does not necessarily tell you about what actually happened.

If your main interest is in the actions or behaviour of people in a particular situation (rather than their thoughts, feelings or attitudes), *observation* may be the best choice of method. Observation may be unstructured: at its most extreme this may involve you in making notes of everything that you notice about what is happening in a situation. The problem about this is that your data may be too complex to handle, making the picture that emerges an incoherent one. One way of getting round this difficulty is to structure your observation. For instance, you might design a schedule to enable you to count the frequency of particular pieces of behaviour. If you use structured observation, you may find that categorising behaviour is not at all straightforward in practice. If this is not recognised in the way you present your findings, you may make your conclusions appear more clear-cut than they are.

The other problem is that, in order to design your schedule, you will probably need to decide what is likely to happen in a situation, or at least what will be the most important categories of phenomena, before you start to observe. This can mean that you interpret everything that happens through your preconceptions and that you miss some important aspects of the situation. Ways of capturing observational data so that you can analyse it in more depth and check your interpretation with others include using video, tape recordings or photographs. Croll (1986) provides a useful introduction to systematic classroom observation.

Diaries and field notes allow you to collect a range of information as it occurs, using any of the techniques described above, in order to analyse and interpret it at a later date (see for instance, Burgess, 1984). You can also ask others to keep diaries for you. This technique allows you to explore phenomena in as natural a setting as possible. On the other hand, it does rely on you (or others) making notes of events as they occur, generally in the course of a busy day, which can be difficult.

Document or systems analysis can be useful for getting at the implicit values that underlie institutional practice and what actually happens at the institutional level. Documents are part of the public face of institutional activity. You might look at the content in terms of what it includes, what is left out. The messages within documents help to define the institution and can affect its strategy, and so the lives of those operating within it. You might also look at the systems within an institution. For instance, you might look at what data is collected by a school or college, in order to see if it can be analysed for interesting trends to reveal particular issues. On the other hand, you might analyse a 'system' (for instance, the admissions process) from the point of view of the client. You could look at the entire process from beginning to end to see who benefits from each element of the process and whose interests and needs are being catered for. From this process, you might be able to suggest changes to make systems more client-centred.

Case study generally involves several techniques so that you can look at a variety of aspects of a situation and explore complex issues. Yin (1989) provides a useful introduction to case study. It is an approach that enables the researcher to use a variety of data collection techniques to look at a variety of viewpoints. Somebody, generally the person who has collected them, has to interpret them. For this reason, case study seldom claims the same sort of objectivity that comes from experiments and surveys. As Yin points out, whilst experiments and surveys usually involve *statistical* generalisation, case studies rely on *analytical* generalisation (p. 39).

The important thing with all research and evaluation is not to make claims for it that cannot be substantiated by the methods you use and the context in which you carry it out. If you are interested in developing as an enquiring teacher, you may find a general introduction to research, such as those written by Edwards and Talbot (1994) or Bell (1993), a useful starting-point for making choices about methodology.

The nature of reliability and validity

Whether you are attempting to undertake a piece of research that you hope will ultimately be published, undertaking a small-scale evaluation to improve your practice or your institution's policy making, or reading educational research in the expectation that it will inform your practice, it is important that you understand that all research methods have their limitations. The first step towards this informed scepticism is to understand issues of validity and reliability. These terms were discussed in chapter 6 in the context of assessment. Below, I describe how they apply to research and enquiry.

Validity asks the big question of whether the researcher is finding out or has found out what they imagine. It is therefore the overarching concept, reliability being a subset of validity. The problem is that there are often tensions between the two ideas. Valid data about (say) classroom processes, often requires the researcher to discover a complex story about one situation, but the data may lack external validity: it may not be generalisable beyond that particular time and place. This data may not be reliable: similar situations or the same situation on another day may not function in the same way, and another observer describing the situation at the same time and place may tell a different story. Nevertheless, the researcher's story may be 'true' or at least describe a recognisable version of the truth. Thus, methods and results may be valid but unreliable (or vice versa).

Brown and Knight (1994) give a good description of the operation of validity and reliability in assessment. The points that they make about reliability can be generalised to other research foci: for instance its relationship to the consistency of measurement or measurements. If you set up a small- or large-scale enquiry, you will need to consider various aspects of this consistency. This does not imply that you have to restrict yourself to data (such as numerical indicators) that are relatively simple to compare, but that may not describe the total setting. If you want to use more complicated measures (such as verbal descriptions or explanations) as part of your data, you may need to consider whether to use triangulation techniques to test your interpretations against those of others. Such techniques include inter-observer agreement, the use of two instruments (for instance, interviews and questionnaires) that purport to measure the same aspect of a situation, or agreements between the same measure (such as test–retest procedures).

Much institutional energy has gone into ensuring reliability of assessment and quality standards in recent years. For example, in the UK, senior staff have been working hard to set up systems to ensure academic standards are monitored and institutional scores (for instance in GCSE examination league tables) improved. Institutions have created policy documents in anticipation of inspection and audit visits that often include measurable performance indicators and the ways that these will be monitored. This is often regarded by OFSTED and others as self-evidently good practice. The professional will question whether this search for reliable measures of performance has sometimes been at the expense of a concern for validity, and whether it is always the case that worthwhile educational objectives can be reliably assessed by such measures. Education changes people in fundamental ways. This may mean that the assessment of higher level of achievement relies on complex judgments which cannot be reduced to one or two numerical dimensions.

Both reliability and validity pose questions about the nature of evidence – its sufficiency, the claims that may be made and the extent to which claims are met – but validity (the question of whether you have measured what you have set out to measure) may be the more pertinent issue for the professional. Researchers are likely to ask fundamental questions about the assumptions and attitudes underpinning the questions asked and categories used by an assessor or researcher and the ways that these have influenced the results and their interpretation. The reflective professional must consider subjectivity as part of the context for educationally and morally defensible action, even if this is not the prevailing educational orthodoxy.

Interpreting research and enquiry reports

Ridgeway (1992) discusses the political context of teaching competence and its effect on the reliability and validity of assessments. Much of this analysis applies more generally to research and evaluative data collected by teachers for a whole variety of purposes. As a professional, keen to gain knowledge and insights into your actions by reading relevant educational research, you will need to develop skills of critical analysis and knowledge about factors that commonly jeopardise different kinds of research.

Research in education may fall into the quantitative tradition and focus on the collection (usually of large amounts) of numerical data, or into the qualitative tradition and look in depth at a smaller number of instances. It may be focused on 'discovery' or on the improvement of practice. There is much ideological baggage that now surrounds these traditions in education. The professional will need to understand something of this debate in order to assess the value position of a particular piece of research, and its potential relevance to her or his own situation.

Within education there has been a shift from models of research based on the positivistic tradition of experimental and quasi-experimental research methods, towards interpretative, descriptive methods within naturalistic settings, described as 'ethnographic' methods. Each of these models has its weakness. There is a tendency for the positivistic tradition to give more credence to quantitative data and the interpretative one to value qualitative methods and data. The interpretative tradition is characterised by limited scope, particularity and subjectivity, the positivistic tradition by the triviality of some its findings and difficulties in application to the classroom. Bassey (1990) gives a very clear explanation of these paradigms and their characteristics and also contrasts them with action research.

It is important that the professional appreciates that each type of research should be judged in its own terms. For instance, questions of usefulness or applicability may not be to the point of some types of quantitative research, which may be aiming to inform debate or test the strength of a hypothesis that has general acceptance. It is sometimes as a result of such research that taken-for-granted assumptions about educational reality become challenged. Quantitative research is 'good' research if the results are valid and reliable.

Research in the qualitative tradition must also be judged by appropriate criteria. It should not be criticised for subjectivity, unless it makes claims to be objective. In research that is problem-centred and pragmatic, the notion of proof becomes irrelevant. The validity of such research depends on the extent that the situation, actions, causes and effects are described convincingly. In assessing its quality from your point of view, you may need to look out for interjudgmental reliability (do the reader, researchers and the actors in the research situation describe and interpret the findings in the same way?); pragmatic considerations (was the problem solved to the satisfaction of all?); and its congruence with the values that underpin professional practice (the moral basis of actions by the researcher – did they ask the right question, were they open about their thoughts, feelings and motives, were the values that underpinned the research made explicit?).

Each of the traditions makes its own assumptions about cause and effect. The quantitative tradition presupposes that the truth can be ascertained with some degree of objectivity. The qualitative tradition accounts more easily for the thoughts, feelings and assumptions of the participants in education. One model simplifies reality in order to look at and analyse it. In the other, more of the complexity of reality is explored (although data generally have to be simplified before a coherent picture can emerge). The qualitative tradition tends to be inductive and the qualitative tradition, deductive. Maybe the best research studies will use some aspects of each.

As a reader of research, you need the tools to help you determine whether the results are, or are not, relevant. Quantitative research methods in education may claim relevance because of some kind of objectivity or because the 'test' used has been found to work similarly in other situations. External validity (the extent that the results of a study can be generalised to other times and places) generally derives from the situation and population studied: the size of sample, its 'typicality' and the categories used. Internal validity depends upon control of the variables in the situation and whether the number of instances of a particular result can be considered significant. Statistical significance is determined by a standard statistical test, which usually aims to help the researcher to look at how scores are distributed and to make judgments about the role of chance in how the scores 'fall'. (See Campbell and Stanley (1963) for more about validity in quasi-experimental research.)

When reading research from the qualitative tradition, in order to answer the question, 'Might this research have some significance to me in my particular situation?', you may need to know the author's claims to expert knowledge, the extent to which his or her conclusions and interpretation of the situation have been tested against the interpretations of other parties, the assumptions that the researcher made, and his or her emotional responses to issues examined. Elliott (1991) provides a good account of the strengths and weaknesses of research within the qualitative research tradition.

If you are interested in developing as a professional, I have suggested that you will not only wish to read research intelligently but also to engage in enquiry in order to evaluate the effects of your actions. The kind of insider research that may be most appropriate to reflective practice may use experimental methods and 'soft' quantitative techniques, but usually relies more on the qualitative research tradition.

Ethical issues in research and enquiry

It is important to recognise that all research instruments have in-built error, but that the nature of this error varies between instruments. While some people might still insist that the only good educational research is that which attains some kind of value-freedom, I believe that the educational, moral, philosophical and political values that underpin research into professional practice are basic to its quality. If this is an issue that concerns you, when reading research you may need to look at the source of the research and the extent that the researcher(s) may have a vested interest in a particular set of results (perhaps because the results show them to have been successful innovators, or because they have a particular political perspective that they wish to promote). Without a notion of educational and moral defensibility, there are opportunities for distortion in most educational research and evaluation: for instance, scores for student achievement can be raised (or lowered), without any changes in actual learning, by subtle adjustment to assessment tasks, processes or context.

The issue of confidentiality is an important one in research. This can be in relation to the way that data is collected and kept, as well as how it is written up. You need to be careful about who might catch sight of your raw data, how you classify what you observe or notice, and with whom you discuss your data. All respondents in research and others who might be affected, are entitled to be consulted on issues of confidentiality. This applies to students, children and their parents, as well as to others involved, and it applies irrespective of the relative power of those affected by the research. The relatively powerful (for instance, managers within an institution) have rights as far as the questions you ask about them and of them, as well as the less powerful. The point is that all data must be attained ethically, analysed ethically and reported ethically.

You also need to think carefully about the institution and its rights over the way you report what is going on. You may need to make considerable efforts to avoid identifying a particular institution that is included in your research. This can be a particular problem in insider research, where the identity of the subjects of the research and the nature of its context can be fairly obvious. In this case, the ground rules concerning the conduct of the research, its nature, how it will be disseminated, and who will be given a right of veto should be very carefully thought through and made explicit to all concerned.

Issues of confidentiality are perhaps more important in researching education than in some other fields. This is because many of the respondents are relatively powerless, but it is also due to the nature of the data we are collecting. In educational settings, much of this will describe the 'subjective realities' of people and the relationships between them. We may find we are uncovering matters which normally remain hidden from view. Confidentiality is likely to figure in our assurances to those we question and in the way we protect our sources in reporting. It is important, whether our research is qualitative, quantitative, inductive or deductive.

In research based on positivistic assumptions, ethical issues are sometimes not seen as being intimately bound up in all aspects of the research. This puts a particular onus on you, as a professional enquiring into practice, or as a reader of research, to consider carefully the extent that the research conforms to ethical principles.

It is a fundamental principle of all educational research that those involved should not be harmed by the process or results. Harm can sometimes take forms that are not immediately obvious. You need to be very vigilant. For instance, a research student with whom I worked was interested in how boys, who seemed to be part of an under-achieving sub-culture within a school, might describe themselves as learners. To begin with, it seemed straightforward to ask them about this in a group situation. However, on reflection, she wondered whether such a discussion, without any attempt on her part to mediate the boys' attitude, might not reinforce the negative or stereotyped labels that some of them applied to themselves as male students. She wondered whether she should speak to them individually, and if she did so, what she should do about any negative attitudes that emerged. It seemed to her that her duty as a professional meant that her research could not merely discover the problem, but once a problem became uncovered, she must seek to improve the situation. Another student had a problem in seeking to set up a quasi-experimental research design using a control group. Since his experimental group would be subject to an educational programme intended to promote their learning, he felt that it would be harmful to deny the control group the potential benefit. His consideration of the ethics of the situation, led him to modify his research design and move away from an experimental model altogether.

As a professional it is necessary to consider your own values in relation to the focus, methods and dissemination of research. The principles that underpin reflective practice assume a disposition to enquire into the congruence between your action and your values. This implies that you make your values, and your implicit theories of action, explicit. These principles should also inform the methods and approach that you take to enquiry. For instance, if you are interested in empowering your students, it does not make sense to treat them as 'subjects' in your research. At the minimum, you will want to ensure that your students are well-informed about what you are planning, what use you might make of your enquiry and how the results are actually used. For this reason, I generally publish the results of the staff evaluations of my performance as a manager (collected through confidential questionnaires) that I regularly carry out, together with some indications of areas of my performance that I intend to work on as a result. You may wish to go further than this and include your students (or others that you involve in your enquiry) as partners in research. This would imply that you might involve them in helping to define your research question or focus in a way that is relevant to them. They might help you to design research instruments and validate your interpretation of the results. This approach may be particularly important for those groups that traditionally have been disempowered, and subject to professional action – to the expert knowing best – such as people with learning difficulties.

It can be useful to look at one of the statements of ethical principles underlying research, such as that produced by the British Educational Research Association, in order to check that you have considered as many ethical issues as possible before you embark upon a piece of research or an enquiry.

Conclusion

The creative professional takes their responsibilities as a teacher seriously. They are continuously striving to improve their practice. This striving involves trying to find solutions to problems, or approaches that transform their nature through imaginative thinking. It also involves the stimulus and evaluation of improvements through systematic enquiry into the teachers' assumptions, perceptions and practice, and those of other stakeholders in the educational process, particularly the students' learning and experience.

References

ARGYRIS, C. and SCHÖN, D. (1974) *Theory into Practice: Increasing Professional Effectiveness*, London: Jossey-Bass.

ASHCROFT, K. (1987) 'The history of an innovation', *Assessment and Evaluation in Higher Education*, **12**, 1, pp. 37–45.

ASHCROFT, K., BIGGER, S. and COATES, D. (1996) *Researching Equal Opportunities in Colleges and Universities*, London: Kogan Page.

ASHCROFT, K. and FOREMAN-PECK, L. (1994) *Managing Teaching and Learning in Further and Higher Education*, London: Falmer Press.

ASHCROFT, K. and FOREMAN-PECK, L. (1996) 'Quality standards and the reflective tutor', *Quality Assurance in Education*, **4**, 4, pp. 17–26.

BASSEY, M. (1990) 'On the nature of research in education', *Research Intelligence*, **36**, 37, 38, pp. 35–44.

BELL, J. (1993) *Doing your Research Project: A Guide for the First-time Researcher in Education or Social Science* (2nd Edition), Buckingham: Open University Press.

BENNETT, C., HIGGINS, C. and FOREMAN-PECK, L. (1996) *Researching into Teaching Methods in Colleges and Universities*, London: Kogan Page.

BROWN, S. and KNIGHT, P. (1994) *Assessing Learners in Higher Education*, London: Employment Department Development Group.

BURGESS, R. (1984) 'Keeping a research diary,' in BELL, J. and GOULDING, S. (eds) *Conducting Small-Scale Research Investigations in Education Management*, London: Harper and Row.

CAMPBELL, D. T. and STANLEY, J. C. (1963) *Experimental and Quasi-experimental Designs for Research*, Chicago, Il: McNally.

CARR, W. and KEMMIS, S. (1986) *Becoming Critical: Education, Knowledge and Action Research*, London: Falmer Press.

COHEN, L. and MANION, L. (1985) *Research Methods in Education* (2nd Edition), Beckenham: Croom Helm.

CONNOLLY, F. M. and CLANDININ, D. J. (1990) 'Stories of experience and narrative enquiry', *Educational Researcher*, **19**, 5, pp. 2–14.

CORTAZZI, M. (1993) *Narrative Analysis*, London: Falmer Press.

CROLL, P. (1986) *Systematic Classroom Observation*, London: Falmer Press.

DAVIES, S. and HEADINGTON, R. (1995) 'The focus group as an educational research method', *British Educational Research Conference*, Oxford: October.

DEWEY, J. (1916) *Democracy and Education*, New York: The Free Press.

EDWARDS, A. and TALBOT, R. (1994) *The Hard-pressed Researcher; A Research Handbook for the Caring Professions*, London: Longman.

ELLIOTT, J. (1991) *Action Research for Educational Change*, Buckingham: Open University Press.

MARTON, F. and SALJO, R. (1984) 'Approaches to learning' in MARTON, F., HOUNSELL, D. J. and ENTWISTLE, N. J. (eds) *The Experience of Learning*, Edinburgh: Scottish Academic Press.

RAMSDEN, P. (1992) *Learning to Teach in Higher Education*, London: Routledge.

RIDGEWAY, J. (1992) *The Assessment of Teaching Quality*, Lancaster: Faculty of Social Science, Lancaster University.

ROGERS, C. (1983) *Freedom to Learn in the 80s*, Columbus, OH: Charles, E. Merrill.

STENHOUSE, L. (1987) 'The conduct, analysis and reporting of case study in educational research and evaluation' in MURPHY, R. and TORRANCE, H. (eds) *Evaluating Education: Issues and Methods*, London: Harper and Row.

YIN, R. K. (1989) *Case Study Research: Design and Methods*, Beverly Hills: Sage.

ZEICHNER, K. (1982) 'Reflective teaching and field-based experience in teacher education,' *Interchange*, **12**, 4, pp. 1–22.

Further reading

Any of the books in the *Practical Research Series*, edited by Ashcroft, K. and Palacio, D. and published by Kogan Page will provide a variety of starting-points for small-scale research aimed at improving your practice as a teacher.

Bassey, M. (1990) (see above for the full reference).
Provides one of the best synopses of the main approaches to educational research.

Notes on contributors

Kate Ashcroft is Dean of the Faculty of Education at the University of the West of England. She has taught extensively within teacher training programmes for further and adult education lecturers. For many years she worked as a teacher and advisory teacher in schools. She has published several books and numerous papers about teaching, learning and research within post-compulsory education.

Gaynor Attwood is a Principal Lecturer at the University of the West of England. She contributes to the ICT delivery and strategy within the Faculty of Education and manages several projects concerned with the use of new technology in education. She works with teachers and students in relation to ICT in learning, with a particular emphasis on the role of assessment. She is the Chief Examiner for RSA's CLAIT.

Gillian Blunden is currently the Director of Research in the Faculty of Health and Social Care, at the University of the West of England. She has worked in teacher education for a number of years training teachers/lecturers for the post-16 sector and health and social care and adult education lecturers. She has served as the Chair of Governors for a number of school governing bodies. Her major research interest is in the education of healthcare professionals.

David James is Principal Lecturer in the Faculty of Education, University of the West of England. After a variety of manual and non-manual jobs he gained a degree in Social Science at the University of Bristol as a mature student, followed by a Cert. Ed.

(FE). He has taught in further and higher education since 1981, and increasingly in teacher education since 1986. His research interests include student experience, learning and assessment in a range of post-compulsory settings. He completed a PhD in 1996, and is co-author (with Michael Grenfell) of *Bourdieu and Education – Acts of Practical Theory* (1998, Falmer Press).

Marelin Orr-Ewing trained as a secondary teacher of English in the early 1970s and has taught in secondary schools and a college of further education. In 1990 she joined the University of the West of England. She has taught on undergraduate and postgraduate courses and become involved in several of the university's overseas projects. She has also been responsible for delivering the university's professional development programme for new lecturers to teaching and learning in higher education. Marelin is currently the PGCE (secondary) award leader.

Keith Postlethwaite is Head of Research and Staff Development at the University of the West of England. He is involved in teacher education at all levels with special interests in research methods, pupils' individual differences, and science education. He has published extensively in the area of teaching and learning. His current research interests include differentiation in science teaching, and professional learning in education and in other professions.

John Ryan trained as a secondary teacher in the 1970s and taught in secondary schools in London before joining the University of the West of England in the mid-1980s. He has worked on several National Curriculum development projects, including EATE and Economics 16–19.

Lynne Walker is Associate Dean in the Faculty of Education at the University of the West of England. She has held a number of management posts in secondary schools, a local education authority and higher education. She has developed her interest in education management, particularly women and management, through teaching, consultancy, training activities and writing. She is the co-author, with Jenny Ozga, of a number of book chapters and conference contributions on the subject of women in educational management.

Index